M000032005

When God Is Silent

ILLUMINATION
PUBLISHERS

WHEN GOD IS
Silent
The Problem of Human Suffering

DOUGLAS JACOBY

When God Is Silent

The Problem of Human Suffering

Copyright © 2019 by Douglas Jacoby and Illumination Publishers

All rights are reserved. No part of this book may be duplicated, copied, translated, reproduced, or stored mechanically, digitally, or electronically without specific, written permission of the author and publisher.

ISBN: 978-1-948450-32-4. Printed in the United States of America.

Unless otherwise indicated, all Scripture references are from the *Holy Bible, New International Version,* copyright ©1973, 1978, 1984, 2011 by Biblica, Inc. Used by permission. All rights reserved worldwide.

Interior book design: Toney C. Mulhollan.

Cover design: Roy Applesamy.

Illumination Publishers titles may be purchased in bulk for classroom instruction, business, fund-raising, or sales promotional use. For information, please e-mail paul.ipibooks@me.com.

Illumination Publishers cares deeply about using renewable resources and uses recycled paper whenever possible.

Published by Illumination Publishers, 6010 Pinecreek Ridge Court, Spring, Texas 77379-2513. www.ipibooks.com.

About the author: Since 2003, Dr. Douglas Jacoby has been a freelance teacher and consultant. With degrees from Duke, Harvard, and Drew, he has written more than thirty books, recorded over 600 podcasts, and spoken in 125 nations around the world. Douglas is also professor of theology at Lincoln Christian University. In *When God Is Silent,* he digs deep to share both biblically and personally from his first four decades as a follower of Christ. For more about the work and ministry of Douglas Jacoby go to www.douglasjacoby.com.

Table of Contents

IN MEMORIAM

TO THE MEMORY OF
SUZANNE LILLIS JACOBY
1964–1984

Preface

DIVINE SILENCE

In my international Bible teaching ministry, I interact with people all over the globe—in conferences, church and social fellowship, and in universities. I present lessons like "Is There a God?" or "Do All Roads Lead to God?" and "Science & Faith: Enemies or Allies?" Yet probably the most heartfelt objection to God's existence is the presence of suffering in the world. The first time I put the topic of suffering on the program, I wasn't so sure I had made the right choice—until I saw the impact of openly addressing this issue.

The truth is, the problem of human suffering is a key area of Christian evidences. Because of the suffering they have witnessed (or experienced) on the planet—some of it pure evil—far more people question how there can be a good God than wonder whether the Bible has been copied accurately, or whether miracles really happen. Pain and suffering are intrinsic parts of earthly life, and as we shall see, they play crucial roles in our personal development.

One reason I was drawn to Christianity is that the biblical message rings true. The Christian faith is realistic. It offers no facile solutions to the problem of human suffering—nor shall I attempt to offer easy answers in this book. Christ does, however, offer grace, comfort, and strength so that in the face of suffering we may live with dignity, poise, and purpose.

The words "when God is silent" may remind the seasoned Bible reader of Job, or perhaps one of the Psalms touching on divine silence.[1] Is not divine silence what Jesus Christ experienced on the cross, prompting him to pray these words of David?

> *My God, my God, why have you forsaken me?*
> *Why are you so far from saving me, from the*
> *words of my groaning?*
> *O my God, I cry by day, but you do not answer,*
> *and by night, but I find no rest.*

(Psalm 22:1–2 ESV)

Of course, the Father never abandoned the Son. Even though he cried out on the cross, the Lord was not selecting isolated phrases that captured his feelings, but praying a psalm—one that spoke of a whole series of events. The psalm not only overflows with anguished emotions of pain, but also with the confident expectation of deliverance (see v.22).

While we are not Jesus Christ, we inhabit the same world he did—one of pain, joy, surprise, suffering, and wonder. At times life is good, joyous, and fair. At other times it's dreary, unfair, and hard. We may pray with little sense that God is listening. In many ways, divine silence is part of this life. It can be deeply unsettling when we have been wronged, misrepresented, defrauded, violated, or betrayed. Inwardly or perhaps vocally, we cry out for divine justice. To hear nothing in response is difficult, even disorientating.

After my publisher and I had settled on our title, we discovered *seventeen* other works also called *When God Is Silent*[2]—and many more similarly named. Surely this is an indication of both the pervasiveness of human suffering and the importance of our theme. Regardless of our experience, culture, or geographical location, none of us is shielded from suffering.

The problem of suffering troubles us always, and that is unlikely to change just because we read a book. But at least we can make progress. To some questions there are well-defined answers; to others, only further questions. Regardless, the goal is a more balanced and biblical perspective.

Thank you for allowing *When God Is Silent* to play a small role in this process.

Douglas Jacoby
Ashdod, Israel
2 November 2018

1. Job 34:29; Psalm 28:1; 35:22; 39:12; 50:3; 109:1—and certainly 88:1–18.

2. A list we compiled from Amazon.com includes works by Gloria Burgess, Patrick Carter, Lilliet Garrison, Ike Idegbama, Kellie Lane, James Long, Raul Marrero, Luis Martinez, Emmanuel Okose, Daniel Okpara, D. K. Olukoya, Simon Olulade, Charles Swindoll, Barbara Taylor, Elmer Towns, and Bob Yandian. (I assume there are more.) Consider also the following from *Christianity Today* (CT):

    "At CT, we publish more pieces about God and suffering than perhaps any other topic. It's arguably the biggest question that humans ask of faith. We know at least anecdotally that in times of disproportionate evil—think post-World War I Europe—waves of people turn from God. And data suggest that, in recent decades, the problem of evil is increasingly cited as the chief reason for abandoning faith." From "Say That Again: When it takes more than one story to tell a story," by Andy Olsen, Managing Editor, *Christianity Today*, July/August 2018.

Chapter 1

Two Types of Pain

I cried because I had no shoes
until I met a man who had no feet.
—Old Persian saying

There was a faith healer of Deal,
Who said, "Although pain isn't real,
When I sit on a pin
And it punctures my skin,
I dislike what I fancy I feel."

Pain is part of life, from birth all the way to death. Sometimes it is minor—like my physical discomfort on a recent flight to the West Coast. I was jammed between the curve of the plane's fuselage and my fellow passenger, into whose territory my shoulder intruded for a full five hours. At other times pain is nontrivial—broken limbs, kidney stones, migraine headaches, back injury, childbirth.

Before we begin our exploration of divine silence in the face of human suffering, it may help to step back and survey the types of pain we all experience. Broadly speaking, there are two categories of pain, *physical* and *emotional.* Which is worse? I find that young people usually answer, physical pain. But the older we get, the more our experiences teach us that emotional pain is much worse as it last much longer.

Although no one *wants* to have their arm broken, many of us will have broken bones in the course of our lifetime, just as we also can expect a variety of emotional hurts. Consider these two scenarios.

> *Option 1*
> You stumble and fall, and your arm is broken. At the hospital, the bone is reset and put in a cast, and you are told to come back in six weeks to have the cast removed. You will regain full use of your limb.

> *Option 2*
> Your best friend betrays you, your spouse leaves you, and a horrific accident befalls one of your children. All you can do is endure it—your thoughts chaotic— pulsing with emotional pain.

Would you hesitate to declare which scenario is more painful? Offered a choice, most mature people, I am sure, would say, "Just break my arm!" Because the truth is, pain of the heart is far more serious than bodily pain; it is hurt and distress seemingly without limit. Our Lord nobly endured physical pain for us, but the emotional pain he endured *daily*—not only in his passion—is unfathomable.

Broken Toes

Physical pain can be agonizing, but rarely does it rank in severity with emotional pain. A few years ago I broke my toe. Barefoot, I was walking too quickly in my house—or at least that is what my wife would say—and kicked the doorframe. I would say that the house was designed with the doors too narrow. (My shoulders barely clear the sides of the doorframe—my excuse for the digital fracture.) After that injury, I walked with a cane, managing just fine.

By the autumn of that same year, Vicki and I had walked coast to coast across England.[1] The pain (aches, blisters, cuts, bleeding) was trivial, especially in light of the goal. I never thought, "Oh my, this reminds me of the time when I broke my toe!" Not at all.

A month later, I twisted my ankle badly and had to use a cane for two months. (I was doing extreme sports: nocturnal dog walking.) The pain did not remind me of *all* the physical injuries I had ever experienced. No, we start afresh each time we experience physical pain—it isn't cumulative. Not so with emotional pain.

Broken Hearts

I learned this one year when I suffered a lot of emotional pain. I was forced to resign from my job (after twenty years in church ministry). A few months later, my father died of cancer. The family had had a heads-up, with several months of medical visits, unsuccessful surgery, and physical deterioration. We were not emotionally close, and so I had assumed that when he passed this would not be a painful time for me.

The night before the funeral, I was talking with one of my father's friends, and I began to feel pangs of grief. The next morning, my brother and I offered the eulogy. Steve spoke well, but I could hardly finish through all the tears. I reminisced about what it was like when I was a little boy, recounting the happy times, like when my dad would carry me on his shoulders. He was tall, and I loved to reach up high. In our nightly routine I would touch the top of every doorway as he carried me to bed. Then there was the smell of his aftershave and the feel of his beard on my cheek at the end of the day. When I expressed these things, I burst into loud sobs. (Our kids had never seen me weep.) I had reasoned (perhaps like you) that if you are not close to someone, it won't hurt so much when they die. I was wrong.

But there was more to come. Two months later, the son of the man who had helped me become a Christian took his own life. My family had just relocated from Australia to the United States, to the town in which the young man leaped to his death. We were grateful to be there to offer support to his father, mother, and brother. This was the saddest I'd felt all year. In terms of pain, the job loss was sobering, Dad's death hurt more, but the suicide caused a most profound sadness. I later realized the consecutive losses created a crescendo—piercing, *cumulative* pain.

RECAP

- Pain is a normal part of life.
- There are two broad types of pain, emotional and physical.
- Emotional pain is usually the more serious of the two.
- Pain is often cumulative (especially the emotional kind).

---

1. As Great Britain is not that wide, it is no great feat to hike coast to coast. We followed Hadrian's Wall, constructed by the Romans in AD 122, ostensibly to keep the Scots out of England. At fourteen miles a day, we crossed the country in six days. (The path is 84 miles, or 136 km.)

Chapter 2

Sources of Suffering

I am my own worst enemy—
Somebody save me from myself.[1]

A 100

Pain and suffering have many causes. As we strive for a biblical perspective on the problem of suffering,[2] it will help to consider these sources.

Our Own Worst Enemy

How do we make sense of the evil, pain, and suffering in the world? We never will—at least completely—but most of us make the effort. No comprehensive discussion of God's justice can omit the topic of free will and the choices we make. Most of the pain, both physical and emotional, that I have suffered in my life has been caused by *me*. I don't need a philosopher or a theologian to explain it to me.

The relationships I have ruined, the things I have done to the people I love—who am I to blame for that? My dad was not emotionally close to me during his lifetime. His father before him was not close to him, either. I could blame it on the

18

previous generations. But we must own up to our actions and their consequences.

My Own Self-Inflicted Pain (Physical)

- In the diving test for the swimming merit badge (Boy Scouts), I shredded my knees on the edge of the dock instead of diving over it. Lots of blood.

- I'd been working underneath our house in Australia, when I stood up too soon, driving a nail into my (numb)skull. Again, lots of blood.

- On exiting a church building in Lesotho (Africa), I stepped right into a 1m (3') ditch, even though the brothers had warned me. (It was pitch black outside, and the lone light bulb in the parking lot had gone out.) The broken leg I suspected ended up being only a ripe bruise.

Emotional Pain I Have Inflicted

- Stealing my best friend's girlfriend at our high school senior prom. No blood—but in hindsight, deep shame. It ruined our relationship and tainted my reputation among classmates.

- Failing to protect my wife in a harsh leadership climate. It's one thing to suffer abuse, another to allow someone you love to unnecessarily endure it.

- Humiliating a young Christian leader publicly. No excuse! (I was a young leader myself, but still should have known better.)

Maybe you are not as clumsy or insensitive as I am, but we all suffer or inflict pain, and most of this is our own dumb fault! Once when I was in the chapel of Harvard Divinity School, I came across an old hymn. I have never forgotten these lines, which concisely captured my own frustration with myself:

> God, harden me against myself,
> The coward with pathetic voice
> Who craves for ease, and rest, and joy.
> Myself, arch traitor to myself,
> My hollowest friend, my deadliest foe,
> My clog whatever road I go.[3]

Aren't we all our own worst enemy? We must take responsibility for what we do to ourselves, and not blame God.

Suffering Caused by Others

When someone brings up Marxism or Nazism, what do we know about these ideologies? Less is said of Karl Marx, but we do talk about Hitler and World War II. Between Hitler and Stalin (including the Soviet *Gulag*), more than 200 million people died last century.

Knowing that, it is hard to deny the incredible power of ideas, the things we have been exposed to in high school, in college, and by reading books. Think about it: this incredible power that God allows us, through our own will and minds, has been used to do much more for harm than for good in every generation.

Consider the evil of terrorism. *Humans* are responsible, not God. After moving to England in 1982 to take part in a church planting, I lived in English dormitories for four years. But for the first few days, my lodgings were in Tavistock Square. When I mention 7/7, most people in the US draw a blank, whereas if I said 9/11, everyone would have something to say. Well, the UK had their "9/11" on July 7, 2005, a day of multiple suicide bombings in London. In one of them, a bus exploded in Tavistock Square, yards from where I lived. Similarly, millions were touched by the coordinated bomb attacks on the public transport system in Spain, and by acts of terror in Germany, France, Belgium, Indonesia, and many other countries. Recalling these events moves us from the philosophical to the profoundly personal.

Or consider our poor stewardship of the environment. Oil spills, radiation leaks, carcinogenic effluents in rivers—is that God's doing? Is he responsible for what we do to ourselves chemically? Do you smoke? When I was a Boy Scout, someone left half a pack of cigarettes lying around, and I "smoked" it out of curiosity, and a little stupidity. (I lit up and smelled the smoke, but didn't suck it down into my lungs.) Yet I am no different from a chain smoker; I just mistreated by body in different ways. Most of us have some measure of self-destructive tendencies.

DEATHS DUE TO ATHEIST IDEOLOGIES (20TH CENTURY)

* 39 million killed in war
* 167 million killed in state-sponsored violence

Permission vs. Creation

God is obviously not responsible for every human choice. Consider the famines that occur throughout the world. We know there is enough food available to feed everyone. Yet we also know that in a lot of countries, due to poor governance and corrupt leadership, food is not available to those in need. Isn't it due to human selfishness that people lose out on their fair share?

Although he already knows the things that are going to happen, God permits them to occur. That God permits evil does not mean that he has created it. This topic we will explore in the next chapter.

Drunken Pilot

I'm on airplanes a lot—usually ministering in fifteen or twenty countries a year. More often than not, passengers are relaxed, the mood pleasant. We put a lot of faith in the pilots up front. But would we have an agreeable trip if the captain (sounding tipsy on the intercom) invited us all to free drinks, along with the crew, "so we can all enjoy ourselves together"? Would you feel secure—or the opposite? These are, after all, the ones supposed to be in charge, responsible for everyone arriving at their destination safe and sound. If we can't trust them, it's a case of more than mere existential angst. And if we couldn't trust God—if he were mean or capricious or inept—all would not be well in the universe!

> *Then Abraham approached him and said: "Will you sweep away the righteous with the wicked? What if there are fifty righteous people in the city? Will you really sweep it away and not spare the place for the sake of the fifty righteous people in it? Far be it from you to do such a thing—to kill the righteous with the wicked, treating the righteous and the wicked alike. Far be it from you! Will not the Judge of all the earth do right?"*
>
> (Genesis 18:23–25)

In Genesis 18 God is about to destroy the righteous with the wicked because the outcry is so great against the people of Sodom and Gomorrah. What was the sin of these cities? It was not sodomy—that was more a symptom than a cause. To know the specific sins for which they were destroyed, read Ezekiel 16:49–50. We see that their gravest sins were greed, gluttony, and unconcern for the poor. The Sodomites' lives revolved around pleasure.

Abraham challenges God, "Will not the Judge of all the earth do right?" Why would Abraham care about these ungodly cities? He had family there: his nephew Lot, Lot's wife, and their two daughters. So Abraham pleads with God, "What if there are fifty righteous people in the city?... Will you… not spare the place for the sake of the fifty righteous people in it?" (This makes me think of some of the questions that believers, as well as unbelievers, ask about the judgment and about hell: Am I really supposed to believe this? Is this fair? Is this really what a loving God would do?[4])

Abraham was wrestling with it, just as we do. The Lord says he will not level these cities if fifty righteous people are found. Then Abraham asks whether God would destroy them if there were forty-five righteous, and again the answer is no. Then he asks what if there were forty, and he eventually comes down to just ten. The point is not that eleven was a special number, or nine. Probably no precise numerical percentage rationalizes God's act. Rather, the significance is that *God is fair*. By expressing his doubt to the Lord, Abraham comes to terms with this—to trust once more in God's justice. He comes to understand that, indeed, the Judge of the all the earth will do right. And the fact is, if the Judge of all the earth would not do right, we would all be in trouble!

Secret Fears

Many Christians rarely verbalize fears like the one Abraham expressed. We'd never say that sometimes God seems like an absolute monster. Yet it's not easy reading passages in the Old Testament that tell of God bringing judgment down on his enemies; or New Testament passages like Mark 9:48, where even Jesus talks about a fire that will not be quenched and the worms that will not die—referring to the dead bodies of those who rebelled against God (quoting Isaiah 66:24). Christians would not say they doubt God, because in the church culture that would not be politically correct. But deep down, what do we really think? What if you were drugged with truth serum and then asked the question—what would you admit?

So we see that the process of grappling with the justice of God is hardly exclusive to the unbeliever; it's part of our odyssey as believers as well. Outsiders have reason to struggle with it, yet someone who doesn't believe in God doesn't make him responsible for making life pleasant or pain-free. ("What is there to gripe about? It's a raw deal for everyone—what does it ultimately matter?"[5])

Not all suffering is morally evil; some of it is "bad" in terms of being undesirable, unpleasant, or destructive. God doesn't manage all events in the cosmos. This is true even of our lives. As Ecclesiastes 9:11 notes, "Time and chance happen to them all." The element of the random, which physicists and biologists understand is essential to life's existence and progress, occasionally leads to birth defects, cancer, or even the hazardous weather often (unfairly) called "acts of God." (We return to this subject in Chapter 5.)

The Most Personal Source of Evil

The issue is not just why bad things happen or why God allows bad people to do bad things, but why *good* people do bad things. We're not as different from the criminals as we might like to think. A robust doctrine of sin (along with a modicum of humility) helps us to come to terms with this reality.

So what's the most personal source of suffering in our world? *We are*—you and I (if we will be honest).

RECAP

- Much of our suffering is self-inflicted.
- Other suffering is caused by fellow humans—not by God.
- All suffering and pain in the world is either caused by or permitted by God.
- Even the most faithful grapple with the justice of God in all this.
- Although there are other sources of suffering (to be discussed later), we are more responsible than we may like to admit. ⚶

In the next chapter we will move in a somewhat more philosophical direction.

---

1. Robert Pettersson, "My Own Worst Enemy," RamPac Recordings, 2011.

2. Theologians speak of theodicy. *Theós* is the Greek word for God, and *diké* is "justice." Given all the suffering we see, how do we defend God's justice? Theodicy is the subject of the book of Job.

3. Amy Beatrice Carmichael (1867–1951).

4. To explore the nature of hell, including implications for the justice of God, see https://www.douglasjacoby.com/heaven-hell-terminal-punishment/. See also the appendix of my little book *What Happens After We Die?* (Spring, Texas: IPI, 2006). The position is also considered from multiple angles in chapter 8 of my *What's the Truth About Heaven and Hell?* (Eugene, OR: Harvest House, 2013—now available at www.ipibooks.com).

5. As a believer in God and in his word, I know that one day he *will* deal with sin, pain, and suffering, and in a decisive way. It is my understanding that when he does, it will be the end of life as we know it—and most of us are not ready for that to happen just yet. I know I am not psychologically ready. I am not sure I want to cross over right now.

Chapter 3

The Atheist's Objections

"Would you discredit my justice?
Would you condemn me to justify yourself?"
(Job 40:8)

In this chapter we will squarely face three common notions held by atheists—though I suspect that many believers wrestle with similar thoughts.

Both Good and Omnipotent

Many agnostics and atheists contend that the presence of evil and pain invalidates faith, bringing up examples like 9/11, the concentration camps at Auschwitz and Dachau, and genocides without number. Seeing so much suffering in the world, they reason that if God exists, either he is good (well-intentioned, perhaps) but not all-powerful, or he is all-powerful but not good (because he does not prevent suffering). If God exists, he is not the omnipotent, omnibenevolent being described by the monotheistic religions. However, this argument against the existence of God—or the existence of a good, all-powerful God—is not as strong as it may at first appear.

Following is the classic objection to the existence of God based on suffering.

THE ATHEIST'S FIRST OBJECTION

1. If Christianity is true, there is a good and omnipotent god.

2. Such a god would ensure that we don't suffer.

3. But we do suffer.

4. Therefore, there is no good and omnipotent god.

5. Therefore, Christianity is false.

In my public debates with atheists, I've noticed that they like to play this card. They triumphantly make their point as though atheists are the objective and insightful ones, while believers have never really thought about the subject. But believers have always struggled with this.

Historically speaking, as mentioned in the last chapters, it is men and women of faith who have been most troubled over the problem of evil—not nonbelievers. We wrestle because we believe there is true good and evil in the world. When we ask for God's intervention, wisdom, or comfort and do not receive it or it is much delayed, we experience significant cognitive dissonance. The atheist and agnostic, on the other hand, have no reason to pray. Their complaint about a lack of goodness and justice is unfounded, in a way, since it presumes that there is (or should be) good and justice in the world. But if there is no God, whatever is, just is. We may speak of preferences, but not of *true* good or evil, justice or injustice.

Thoughtful atheists are framing an important question. Their argument is sound: assuming number No. 2 is true, their conclusions follow. Yet their deductions No. 4 and No. 5 are false. The principal weakness of this line of reasoning is No. 2. I doubt they are in a position to know whether No. 2 is correct. Maybe God has good reasons for allowing a certain degree of suffering.

Let us now consider a second objection.

THE ATHEIST'S SECOND OBJECTION

1. If Christianity is true, God is both good and the creator of all.
2. He is the creator of good.
3. He is also the creator of evil.
4. Yet if he created evil, he cannot be good.
5. Therefore the Christian God does not exist *and*
6. Christianity is false.

Did God Create Evil?

Before we address No. 3, we need to contemplate No. 2. Many suppose that God created good. Yet God did not *create* good. Rather, God *is* good. If God created good, that would suggest that there was a time when there wasn't any good. But he is good and has always existed. He is not only that which is good, but that by which all good is defined.[1] As a result, what he created is good (Genesis 1) or "very good" (Genesis 1:31). Goodness is, in a sense, an extension of who God is, his essence. It exists because he exists. But did God create evil? Everything that was created was created by God, but evil *was not created.* Although it may sound strange, evil is not real in the way that good is real.

Consider a simple example. I once went up in a hot air balloon, standing in the gondola basket. There is a fire that jets upward, heating the air in the balloon and causing it to rise. (If you are tall, like me, you are at the risk of having your hair scorched, so you have to duck.) Now what is heat, anyway, but particles in motion? What, then, is cold? Particles that are *not* in motion—simply the absence of heat. Therefore, in reality, cold is not a thing as heat is a thing; cold is the absence of a thing. Heat is real, but in a way cold is not.

When we experience cold, what we are really experiencing is an absence of heat. In its essence, evil is the absence of God's presence. Evil is when we turn away from God. He didn't create it. Therefore, it is not accurate to say that since God created everything he must have created evil. That just does not wash. Evil isn't a thing, it's a choice—one that *we* make exercising our free will.[2]

So we see, in regard to the atheist's second objection, that while we agree with No. 1 and No. 4, on biblical and philosophical grounds we must reject No. 2 and No. 3. Therefore the conclusions No. 5 and No. 6 are false.

Let's now consider one final objection, which is really a variation on the first. Modern militant atheists, like Oxford's Richard Dawkins—probably the best-known unbeliever in the world—along with Daniel Bennett, Sam Harris, and the late Christopher Hitchens, have often made comments like, "There is no God—what kind of a deity would permit stuff like this to happen?"

THE ATHEIST'S THIRD OBJECTION

1. If Christianity is true, God is in control.

2. The world seems to be out of control—life is full of injustice and inequality.

3. Therefore, God must not be in control.

4. Therefore, the Christian God does not exist *and*

5. Christianity is false.

Is God in Control?

It is widely presumed and frequently affirmed, especially in difficult times, that "God is in control." As when we analyze any argument, it's imperative to define terms. If by control we mean authority, then yes (ultimately), everything happens un-

der his watch. He either causes it or permits it. But if by control
we mean management—making things happen, engineering
outcomes—then God is not in control. So we might or might
not affirm No. 1, depending on the definition.[3]

Granted, (2) is true; life is not fair. The good guys often go
unrewarded, while the bad guys get away with murder. On this
point believers and skeptics, theists and atheists agree. But for
nonbelievers, there is no ultimate vindication, no justice. Believers, on the other hand, understand that in the world to come
all wrongs will be righted, and good will be rewarded.

We may grant the veracity of No. 3, provided we have se-
lected a correct (biblical) understanding of "control." But this
the skeptic may not grant. (And therefore the ensuing conclusions are false.) He or she expects God to *do something* about the
evil and injustice in the world. But the skeptic suffers from a
deficit of patience. Protesting for justice doesn't guarantee immediate relief from above. God asks us to wait. We affirm that
God *will* do something. We anticipate a judgment day when he
will awesomely and overpoweringly settle all accounts. In fact,
if there were no final judgment day, then the world *would* be
profoundly unjust.

We may still wonder how much the Lord does intervene
in our world. In the following chapter we will consider the pain
and suffering that stem from so-called "acts of God."

Hypocrisy?

Of course, people who blame God are hypocrites unless
they themselves are striving to defeat evil in the world. Don't

acquiesce in keeping the conversation at an intellectual level. No one has a valid excuse for ignoring the plight of others. Let's not ask, as the expert in the law asked, "And who is my neighbor?" (Luke 10:29). After all, when it comes to our own lives and decisions, *we* are in control.

RECAP

- The classic argument against the existence of God fails because of a false dichotomy. Quite simply, no one is in a position to know that it is God's agenda to remove all suffering and evil from the world.

- God created neither good nor evil. Good is an extension of his essence; evil is merely the absence of good.

- Although God is ultimately in control, he does not control every event. The one who created the world—electrons, protons, energy, physical parameters—does not micromanage.

- Those who blame God on account of suffering—or deny there is a God, given the degree of the world's suffering— are open to the charge of hypocrisy unless they are actively involved in doing something about the problem.

1 . A related concept is the Euthyphro Dilemma: is something right because God commands it, or does God command it because it is right? Read the following article: https://us7.campaign-archive.com/?u=4a5682d4bc 6d3a2ee49519a21&id=3ecbeb34fe. Consider also the famous C.S. Lewis quote: "I believe in Christianity as I believe that the Sun has risen, not only because I see it but because by it I see everything else." C.S. Lewis, "They Asked for a Paper," in *Is Theology Poetry?* (London: Geoffrey Bless, 1962), 164–165.

2. To put it more philosophically, before there was sin in the world, evil was only potential, not actual; it didn't yet exist. In the beginning there was God (good), then a creation (very good), including creatures with free will (also good). Their sinful choices (bad) actualized, or reified, evil. Critics often speculate that our world is not well designed, given such realities as disease, extinctions, and other "evils." But what makes us think God could have made a better world than the one in which we live? Perhaps conditions are already optimized for maximum good and minimum evil.

3. For more on this, see the thoughtful article by Doug Schaefer, "Is God in Control?" at https://www.douglasjacoby.com/q-a-0429-is-god-in-control-by-doug-shaefer/.

Chapter 4

Acts of God?

Again I saw that under the sun the race is not to the swift, nor the battle to the strong, nor bread to the wise, nor riches to the intelligent, nor favor to those with knowledge, but time and chance happen to them all.

(Ecclesiastes 9:11 ESV)

Some suffering is caused not by human sin, but through contact with nature. We live in a dangerous world, with plenty of storms, floods, fires, earthquakes, and so on. Earth scientists assure us that these are all necessary for life to exist on our planet. Meteorological catastrophes are also an inevitable part of our existence. They are necessary concomitants of life on earth. People often aggravate the discomfort and suffering caused by natural disasters by building in flood plains, erecting large structures that cannot withstand seismic tremors, stripping the land of its protective forests, or choosing to live on the side of a volcano. When we take risks like this, we should not blame God when injury or death ensues.

Interestingly, those events for which humans are clearly not culpable the law attributes to deity:

Act of God: An event that directly and exclusively results from the occurrence of natural causes that could not have been prevented by the exercise of foresight or caution; an inevitable accident. Courts have recognized various events as acts of God—tornadoes, earthquakes, death, extraordinarily high tides, violent winds, and floods. Many insurance policies for property damage exclude from their protection damage caused by acts of God.[1]

"Acts of God"?

If there is a good God, why were multitudes killed in AD 79 when Vesuvius erupted, as lava and pyroclastic flows obliterated the towns of Pompeii, Herculaneum, and Stabiae? If you have ever been to Italy, maybe you've seen the plaster casts of those overtaken by the ash or lava. One might protest, "God shouldn't have allowed the volcano to explode. He could have prevented it, so why didn't he?"

Every time I go back to Italy I think about when Vesuvius is next going to blow. It did let off some pressure a little during World War II, but it is currently due to explode in a big way. On the downward slopes and in the city of Napoli, there are somewhere around 1.5 million people. Traffic is already thick. When Vesuvius erupts, what will happen? Many will die. And then what will people be saying? "God, how could you let that volcano erupt?" They will undoubtedly have some complaint to throw at God. But if you build your home right in the path of a lava flow, do you have any right to blame God?

Yet even lava is good. Here are some of the reasons:

It may seem like volcanic eruptions serve no purpose except to destroy everything in their path. Volcanoes, however, offer many benefits for life on Earth. Without volcanic eruptions, farming communities would not be able to grow food, certain building materials would not be available, and our atmosphere would not have its oxygen-rich environment.

Billions of years ago, Earth's atmosphere was composed mainly of silicate vapor. During early volcanic eruptions, carbon dioxide and water vapor were among some of the gases released into Earth's atmosphere. The release of these gases helped Earth form its aerobic atmosphere… Volcanic rocks are filled with minerals that, when broken down, provide plants with rich nutrients. Farmers plant and harvest lush crops in the valleys of volcanoes.

Once magma, or lava, reaches the surface, it cools rapidly. After it has completely cooled, magma solidifies into black rocks, which are used in soap and abrasive cleaning materials. Dried lava is also used to build roads and buildings.[2]

Storms—even superstorms—are essential for the existence of life on our planet, as they regulate global heat balance. Further, topography is as important as weather. If everything were flat, we would all end up dying, the whole earth flooded by water. And—you probably guessed it—floods too are essential for life on our planet. For one thing, they redistribute various life forms, improving the ecosystem and providing balance among aquatic populations. The power of a flood is amazing. In 1972 our family visited a place that had recently experienced a flood, Rapid City, South Dakota. It was stunning to me to see that entire buildings were reduced to rubble.[3] I thought, water can do *that*? Or recall the Christmas 2004 tsunami in the Far East—terrifyingly disastrous, with 280,000 killed. These "acts of God" are an essential physical cost of life in the universe. Many other natural disasters, from tornadoes to hailstorms to wildfires, are also indispensable to life on this planet.

The very earth itself is optimized for life. What is its center? A metal core; and why is that important? It generates the magnetic field around the earth. And why is *that* important? It prevents you and me from being baked by cosmic radiation! Without a metal center in our earth, we would have no technology either, as there would be no metallurgy, and so no electronics. But, of course, that would not really matter, because we'd all be dead anyway.

A Safer, Nicer Universe?

You may ask, "Couldn't God have made a different universe—one less hazardous? If he's all-powerful, why should that be a problem?" Perhaps this question is connected to another: "Couldn't he have made a world where humans didn't sin?" I don't know the answer, but I suspect God could not do that, not because of weakness, but because it would be logically impossible. To give us free will but not to allow us to use that free will is logically contradictory. We would not be free—and freedom is the essence of what makes us human.[4]

Before considering whether we would want God to remove all pain and suffering from the world, remember that most suffering is inflicted by people (war, drunk driving, stealing, lying, and the like), so to completely root out evil, he would have to destroy us! As for evil actions, he would have to overrule our decisions, and we would become preprogrammed puppets. But what about evil thoughts? These, after all, are the source of human wrongdoing. God would have to reprogram us, reducing us to the level of automata. Our hard drives (brains) would have to be wiped clean. Would it really be better to live in a world without choice, without free will? Would we be willing to lose our personalities just so we would never feel pain?

Moral Development

Besides, if God were going to make the world agreeable and pleasant for me, then what about the next guy? Would he get his own world, too? In the end, God would have to create as many worlds as people. Yet this would contradict one of God's chief purposes: relationship. We would never know one another if each of us lived in our own private universe. Ponder this: "The nature of human action and interaction requires a reign of law or orderliness. This predictable order makes it possible to set goals, plan their realization, learn from one's mistakes, and above all interact with other persons to form a community."[5] Christian apologist C.S. Lewis wrote:

> God created things which had free will. That means creatures which can go either wrong or right. Some people think they can imagine a creature which was free but had no possibility of going wrong; I cannot. If a thing is free to be good it is also free to be bad. And free will is what has made evil possible. Why, then, did God give them free will? Because free will, though it makes evil possible, is also the only thing that makes possible any love or goodness or joy worth having.

Moral development is possible only when there is genuine freedom. Constant intervention in our children's lives does not work. They have to learn for themselves to avoid what is harmful, to embrace pain when it leads to a higher good (like homework, household chores, or soreness from exercise). Although we play an essential part in their upbringing, we cannot grow *for* them.

The world is ruled by natural laws, yet we may say, wouldn't it be nice if God would intervene every time a falling object was going to land on someone? Maybe he could tip the earth slightly, or just jiggle it to push the object away. But if he does that, someone else might drown in a flood because of it. The farmer is praying for rain for his crops, but the football team is praying for no rain. A family doesn't want their picnic washed out, while in another part of the world, without rain, thousands will die from drought. It makes me hesitant to even pray about the weather!

Does God really change the weather just because we pray about it? Some may respond in the affirmative, citing James 5:17, "Elijah was a human being just like us, and he prayed, and it didn't rain for three and a half years." That is true, but the point of the passage is to be people of faith who pray. It is not a promise that we can command the elements.

Parking Spaces?

Likewise, will God change the universe just to give us a parking space? This is a running disagreement among men and women of strong faith (such as between my wife and me). I tend to think that God doesn't care terribly much which parking space I find. Think about it: If two equally righteous Christians approach the same parking spot, and both pray for the perfect place, what does God do? Does he miraculously split the parking space in two? Or does he cause someone else to pull out? To which some believers reply, "He could if he wanted to!" Yet the question is not what he *could* do, but what he actually does. To intervene for all the righteous to this degree would require him to continually adjust the whole planet to meet our perceived needs. But what does he do *usually*?

But some Christians, referring to Matthew 10:29, will say, "Yes, but not a sparrow falls to the ground apart from the will of the Father." They continue to Matthew 10:30: "And even the very hairs of your head are all numbered." He knows every single thing that happens to us and every detail of our being, but that does not mean he is orchestrating every insignificant event as it occurs—as though he has to make it up as he goes along!

Cancer

Just consider the low survival rate of some cancers, like lung, brain, pancreatic, or stomach cancer. Many of us know people who battle, or have battled, these cancers. It may even be you. Does God have the power to take away any kind of cancer, to heal completely? I believe he does so a lot, and not just for Christians who pray. There are things that medicine cannot explain.

But what *normally* happens? Does God typically obliterate the cancer about which one has prayed? Statistically, no. The issue is not, can he. Of course he can; he is all-powerful. The question is also not, does he love us? Of course he does, but his love may not involve an agenda that includes removing our sickness. Furthermore, that you are not healed does not necessarily point to a lack of faith. Often, cancer goes into remission or just seems to disappear entirely. I say "often" only because about a third of us get cancer at some point, so remission probably occurs millions of times. Yet most of the time, billions of times, it doesn't. God seems to do nothing, *usually*.

Birth Defects

What about birth defects? Considerable suffering is generated by genetic errors: cleft palate, clubfoot, spina bifida, various types of anemia, and countless others. God's plan for building life includes a complex yet elegant tool: DNA. This is a powerful engine for biological diversity and is the fundamental plan for all life forms on the planet, from bacteria to humans. During cell replication, copying errors in the genetic code sometimes lead to birth defects or even prenatal death. The overall plan is good, and it works well. We are "fearfully and wonderfully made,"[6] but that does not necessarily mean perfectly made.

God is all-wise, and never makes "mistakes"—but then, we are not talking directly about God, but about the system he has brought into existence. That is the world we live in, and yet it is a world that gives opportunities to develop a righteous character (the subject of Chapter 5).

Responding to the Skeptic

So when a skeptic asks why he or she should believe in a God who created evil, you can affirm their point: "You shouldn't. But God didn't create evil." Your friend may concede that most evil and suffering is the consequence of human decisions, but is bound to ask, "What about tsunamis and volcanic eruptions and wildfires?" You can suggest that natural disasters are part and parcel of our world, serving multiple essential functions. If our world weren't so dangerous, there would be no life here. Nor does God usually intervene by changing the laws of nature or insulating us from the consequences of our choices in relation to nature.

Did God really have another option? Could God have created a different world, still conducive to human life—without natural disasters, without the potential of evil? Perhaps not. He could have decided not to create the world at all. Why take a chance on humans, with the potential to devastate their world through corruption, betrayal, war, broken families, pollution, violent crime, and the like?

If this is your question, let me ask another. If you are a parent, why did you opt to have children? Whether we procreate, foster, or adopt, can we be absolutely sure that our little ones will turn out perfectly, or that they will not disappoint us—or even become criminals? No, we cannot be sure—so why do we take the risk? For love, for relationship. The Christian Scriptures teach that God created man so that he could love us. God desired children to love. It's about family. God is good and wants to share his love.

Of course, whether we choose to enjoy that love or to abuse the free will he has given us is our decision.

RECAP

- We inhabit a dangerous planet.

- The powerful forces of nature may appear to wreak havoc—we often speak of "acts of God"—yet there is tremendous wisdom in the physical setup of the cosmos.

- In all likelihood, the physical parameters of the cosmos are optimized for life.

- Although God does answer prayer, he does not interfere in all life events, large or small.

- We may believe that for God, creating humans was worth the "risk"—just as we have children, allowing them choices even when they may lead to harm.

1. *West's Encyclopedia of American Law, edition 2*, s.v. "act of god," accessed at https://legal-dictionary.thefreedictionary.com/act+of+god.

2. From "What Is the Importance of Volcanoes to Life on Earth?" https://sciencing.com/importance-volcanoes-life-earth-10048990.html.

3. https://en.wikipedia.org/wiki/1972_Black_Hills_flood.

4. Scientists often point out that, given each individual's brain chemistry, we may have less free will than we realize. But if no one had any free will—if everything were determined by family of origin, neurochemistry, societal trends, etc.—then we could hardly blame the poor fellow who robs a convenience store. But for every robber, there are thousands of people who are not, even though they have been exposed to the same challenging conditions. (If this were not the case, there might not be any convenience stores left!)

5. Dallas Willard, *The Allure of Gentleness: Defending the Faith in the Manner of Jesus* (New York: Harper One, 2015), 127.

6. Psalm 139:14.

Chapter 5

A Matter of Character

You cannot dream yourself into a character;
you must hammer and forge yourself one.

—James A. Froude (1818–1894)

It is hard for an empty bag to stand upright.

—Benjamin Franklin

(Maxims prefixed to Poor Richard's Almanack, 1757)

No discipline seems pleasant at the time, but painful. Later on, however, it produces a harvest of righteousness and peace for those who have been trained by it.

(Hebrews 12:11)

We often refer to suffering as "bad" or "evil." We tend to fasten onto the inconvenience, the pain, and the short term. Yet there are upsides. In this chapter we reflect on one of the noblest long-term outcomes of suffering: character formation. Character is different from personality. Personality is more or less fixed, as it is genetically preconditioned, while character is built and can also be eroded. As someone quipped, "Character is what we are in the dark."

Severe Trials

Many of the 125 nations I have visited have a traumatic history, including the Democratic Republic of the Congo, an enormous country of over 80 million. The Congo is mineral rich but economically poor.

Even after the genocide of the early twentieth century (10 million killed in the former Belgian Congo), the nation has been through decades of hardship, with dozens of warlords and militias who have taken the law into their own hands, pillaging, raping, and murdering. The region is affected by grinding poverty. With few exceptions, only the major roads are paved. Pollution is out of control. Few have access to decent healthcare, going to the witch doctors instead. The level of corruption is astronomical. The woefully underpaid police are especially dangerous.

After one of my messages, I spoke with a brother whom I would describe as warm, giving, and energetic—tall in stature and broad of smile. I was not surprised that this Christian leader heads up a large campus ministry. Nor was I surprised that he is an excellent song leader, radiating joy into the crowd. The following day I learned that he had lost his young wife only a few months before. She was leading an all-night prayer meeting for university students, when death came—suddenly. I have no doubt that losing his wife broke his heart. But it did not shatter his faith or dampen his zeal to serve others.

The Congo is proof positive that suffering does not have to make us less human or lower in character. How can people have been through so much and yet be so patient, joyful, and appreciative of life in Christ? Christians in my country are not nearly as grateful for what they have. (I know—I'm one of them.)

Many disaster-stricken nations have sobered me, like Haiti, which I visited with a friend the year the nation suffered from a horrendous earthquake.[1] Yet Haiti had long been such a poor country that the earthquake didn't significantly lower overall quality of life. It is still the poorest nation in the Western Hemisphere, and the Haitians continue to suffer from poor infrastructure and corruption. When I saw people in Haiti smiling—grateful and undaunted—it was powerful. For us who enjoy the best of Western culture (and complain when we are slightly inconvenienced), it is shaming.

Character

Think of some of the heroes of the twentieth century whom we admire and respect. I recently visited the house of Nelson Mandela. Mandela spent twenty-seven years in prison, from 1963 to 1990, yet went on to negotiate the end of apartheid and was elected President of South Africa. Mahatma Gandhi championed nonviolent protest against injustices in both South Africa and India. He was jailed many times, mocked, hated (and loved), and eventually assassinated in 1948. Martin Luther King Jr, an American Baptist minister, preached nonviolence against racial injustice and segregation, winning the Nobel Peace Prize in 1964. Familiar with hate speech, beatings, and jail, he was assassinated in 1968. Mother Teresa founded the international Missionaries of Charity in 1950, which by 2012 had grown to more than 4500 sisters who managed orphanages, AIDS hospices, leper hospitals, and charity centers worldwide, most notably in Calcutta, India. These selfless servants don't just inspire us; there is something beautiful about their lives as underdogs who ended up impacting the world.

> Let us pray, not for lighter burdens,
> but for stronger backs.

Sports

We know even from sports that it is inspiring to see the underdog persevere. It is enjoyable to watch when one team looks like they are getting decimated, but they come back and win. Recently I watched a rugby match where the challengers and their fans expected a loss—they were thought to have zero chance of winning.[2] The team's supporters had little faith. Faith was easier for me as an outsider (and rugby ignoramus). The underdog South Africa Springboks narrowly defeated number one New Zealand All Blacks, leaving that team in utter shock. It was inspiring, as all underdog comebacks are.

Athletes exercise, they play a game, and they are bruised and maybe beaten, but that can be good. The most punishing tennis match I ever watched was by far the longest in history, Isner v. Mahut at Wimbledon in 2010. The 183-game match took 11 hours, 5 minutes of play over three days. It was hard to fathom the incredible pressure, persistence, pain, and emotional turmoil they endured![3] Yet it was glorious.

When I first lived in the UK (1982), I organized a football (soccer) team for my international hall of residence. Our players came from all over the world—England, Scotland, Hong Kong, Papua New Guinea, Sierra Leone, the USA, and New Zealand. We had a blast, and I never regretted the pain of all those football matches (even when we lost).

Yet the worst injury I ever got was on the football field. I was running hard, when all of a sudden I heard what sounded like a car backfire, or the crack of a whip—but it was the crack of all the ligaments in my left ankle! The pain was unbelievable. Fortunately, surgery saved the foot—and I have an enormous scar to verify the tale. Scars—especially for men—not only document exploits but are badges of honor. All of us are familiar with this kind of "good pain," one we may share with teammates or fellow athletes. In fact, to suffer pain is part of life, and can lead to our forming strength of character: "We also glory in our sufferings, because we know that suffering produces perseverance; perseverance, character; and character, hope" (Romans 5:3–4).

Empathy

When we have suffered and not grown bitter, but kept our faith in the Lord, we exhibit a purer, more genuine love for other people.

During the Arab Spring uprisings, I was speaking in the

Middle East. It was January 2011 when the riots broke out in Lebanon. I saw the thick smoke of burning tires in the streets there. Soon after I landed in Egypt, things seemed to be spiraling out of control as tens of thousands took to the streets to demand the overthrow of President Hosni Mubarak.[4] The church wanted me to speak on "Why Bad Things Happen to Good People," yet not everyone could attend, as many of the roads were blocked. This was during the unrest, when police were spraying the protesters with water cannons as more and more young people filled the streets.

After teaching for a few days, I was urged by local leaders to head to the airport. That was difficult—few taxis, and streets clogged with protesters, riot police, and soldiers. On arriving I learned that Delta was canceling its Egypt route. I queued up to purchase a ticket to Dubai (there's a nonstop from there to our home city of Atlanta), but when I presented my Visa card the agent said, "Sorry, cash only. The president has shut down the internet." That night I slept on the airport floor. I managed to catch a flight the next morning (I'm still not sure how), and landed in Atlanta that evening.

The following morning, right before I left home for Sunday church, the phone rang. It was Ramses (Egyptian preacher). He was checking to see that *I* was okay! They had been praying for me to make it safely out of Egypt. I was bowled over. They were concerned about me—and my relatively minor inconvenience—while they were facing not only social unrest, but ostracism (for being Christians), death squads, and the normal challenges of living in a large, heavily polluted, and often militantly Muslim city. "Yes, I made it. I'm fine, thanks. How are *you*, Ramses?" He cared about *me*. But what about me—do I have the love of Christ in my heart? Those were my thoughts that Sunday morning.

No Guarantee

At this point a critical qualification must be made. The majority of human beings who suffer catastrophically become discouraged, defeated, or embittered. They do not become better people.

I recall an older man I spoke with on the London Underground. I was searching for a point of connection, hoping he would accept an invitation from a total stranger to a Christian event. "Don't believe in God," he replied curtly. I pressed him a little, and he replied, "Where was God during the War?" This man had seen a lot of suffering during World War II. Like many in Europe, his response to his experience of pain was to allow it to steal his faith. "Can't believe in God—no way." Suffering hardens many individuals, while others grow stronger. But where faith meets a gracious spirit, a silver lining often emerges.

Perspective and Age

Something about our perspective changes with age. After our 1982 London church planting, one of the sisters reached out to an elderly man, in his late eighties, who resided in a senior citizens' home. Daniel was Jewish, but this did not deter in the least the sister who invited him. He became a brother in Christ, faithful for the last ten years of his life.

One day my wife and I invited Daniel to our flat for lunch.

His right arm was crippled, permanently doubled at the elbow, with his wrist bent and his hand laid against his chest. He had a shuffling, limping gait and a raspy voice.

I worked up my courage to inquire, "Daniel, what happened to your arm, may I ask?" He responded with a grunt, then said it had happened a long time ago. I asked him if it had happened at work. "Yeah, at work," he rasped. So I asked him, "How old were you when you had the accident?" "I was a young man." "How young?" "Fifty." For Daniel, fifty was young! How perspective changes with age! Generally speaking, the younger we are, the more impatient—and the more perplexed by suffering.

Time has a way of putting suffering into perspective. Imagine living our full "threescore years and ten" (Psalm 90:10 KJV) in a state of perpetual medical agony—fighting arthritis, migraines, ulcers, cancer, or another form of horrible suffering. Seventy years of pain. But compare that with an eternity with God that awaits us after death. That is the biblical perspective: when we die, our suffering ends, and we are forever with our Heavenly Father.

Conclusion

Suffering can lead to significant positive emotional development. Of course, it does not always make people stronger or better, especially in the absence of faith. Rather, pain borne for Christ's sake empowers us to be conformed to the character of Christ. The change isn't automatic; just surviving pain and complaining about it won't improve your heart; it may even degrade it. The operative word is *perseverance* (Romans 5:3–4).

The apostle Paul reminds us that, in accordance with God's will, perseverance through suffering pro¬duces character.

Were it not for pain and suffering in our earthly lives, bravery, heroism, and even stamina would be meaningless. We would live in a soft, mushy world without challenge or thrill. Someone put it well: "God promises a safe landing, not a calm voyage."

In our next chapter we will continue to contemplate the upside of pain and suffering. In our final chapter, "Cruciform Life," we will supply a deeper theological foundation for the connection between suffering and virtue.

RECAP

- Not all suffering is evil; although mistreatment by others is a major cause, sports and hard work entail suffering as well.

- Yet suffering, including what is truly evil, affords an opportunity: the building of character.

---

1. At a minimum, 100,000 lost their lives in the January 2010 quake.

2. No. 1 New Zealand lost to no. 7 South Africa 34-36, on 15 September 2018, in Wellington.

3. A sports surgeon was quoted as saying the players had risked dehydration, hyperthermia, and kidney damage during the long match, and that one or both might suffer "some sort of injury or persistent problem over

the next six months [...] shoulder problems, tendonitis, and recurrent knee problems," as well as the inability to "get into a groove" mentally for up to a year. Gordon Mackay, "Heroic duo John Isner and Nicolas Mahut now face injury risks," *The Scotsman*, 25 June 2010. The twelve next-longest matches of all time all lasted only six or seven hours. https://www.cbssports.com/tennis/news/insane-john-isner-vs-kevin-anderson-wimbledon-match-left-tennis-fans-stunned-and-frustrated/

4. The headlines in the January 26, 2011 papers declared, "The Day of Rage: Thousands clash with police as protests boil over on streets of Egypt and Lebanon." Others called it "The Friday of Anger."

Chapter 6

Power in Pain

> No pain, no palm; no thorns, no throne;
> no gall, no glory; no cross, no crown.
> —William Penn (1644–1718)

We use duct tape to fix everything;
God used nails.

A few years ago, a conference brought me to Orlando, Florida. I stood on a long stage, and as my presentation was finished, people wanted to talk. I didn't feel like walking the distance from center stage around to the side where the stairs led to the seating area. I thought, "I'll just jump down from here." My landing wasn't quite as I anticipated. It was only a few feet to the floor, but I didn't flex my knees the way I should have. The truth is, I was just too old, and I landed hard on my heels. It was agony.

But was it evil? Was there no upside? Our dislike of pain doesn't prove there's something evil about it. In fact, pain can be good. There is power in pain. Let's unpack the concept, first taking the nervous system as an example (that same nervous system that sounded a painful alarm after I jumped off the stage.) We all have one, and that is a good thing. Without a nervous system, what would happen would *not* be good.

The neurologically impaired—those who cannot feel pain—run the risk of grave injury. For decades doctors have known of a rare condition in which children are born without the ability to feel pain. Their parents wish they did have the ability, because the children rarely live long enough to escape their self-inflicted injuries.[1]

Pain gives us a signal: *"Don't go there. It's not good!"* This is why leprosy (Hansen's disease) is so insidious. It eradicates sensation in body extremities. But when people don't feel pain, if they get a cut or wound—maybe a dirty nail goes through the skin on their foot—the wound spreads, because they don't feel it, and so they don't address it. Injured over and over, fingers and toes easily succumb to infection and may even fall off. Infection is particularly dangerous in the body's soft tissues, like those in the area of the eyes. This is why lepers are often blind. The eyes go, and the nose is terribly deformed. Leprosy is rare in modern Western nations, but it is a reality for many unfortunate souls around the world.

If lepers were able to feel the pain initially, they might seek treatment right away. The tragedy is that the disease is easy to cure in the early stages, with just a few dollars' worth of medication, but since it could start with just a small patch on the skin, often by the time treatment is sought, it is too late. If not treated early, the damage is done, and it spreads until *Mycobacterium leprae* runs its course.

A heads-up from a properly functioning nervous system pays off. We eat when we are hungry, although, in the United States at least, sometimes we eat more than we need to satisfy our hunger. What would happen if we didn't feel "stuffed"? We might just keep eating, and eventually, as in the intense crime thriller *Seven*, our stomachs would rupture.[2] As long as the food continued to taste good, what would stop us from keeping on shoveling it in?

Pain has a necessary function in many ways, including in physical and even emotional development. Emotionally, because in social settings we can get signals that tell us, "Tread lightly here," "Don't push that person," "Don't treat people this way." If we don't pick up on those signals, we end up hurting others and ourselves.

And, as we have seen, God brings good from evil. Many Christians love Romans 8:28: "And we know that in all things God works for the good of those who love him, who have been called according to his purpose." That there is a silver lining to every cloud may be too simplistic a perspective on this verse. The apostle Paul did not end there. Romans 8 is about living victoriously in the Holy Spirit, but it is *also* about suffering.

Paul continues in verse 29 (which explains verse 28): "For those God foreknew he also predestined." Many chafe at this point with, "That's not fair. God already chose who would be saved!" No, this passage is not about who will be saved (as the Calvinists imagine). Paul is talking about a different kind of predestination.

Romans 8:28, Partly Understood

In Romans 8, Paul discussed suffering and persecution (vv.17–18, 35). When we experience pain or trouble, Romans 8:28 is often applied like a bandage over a cut. Our friends may aim to console us, "It's all for the good," or "God has a plan." This appeal to Romans 8 is usually intended to make us feel better about the pain. We may hear that something really good will happen to outweigh our suffering, or that our financial losses will be reversed, or that God's ways are mysterious, his providence ever protecting us.

There's some truth in such comments, but look at the broader context. In Romans 8:29, God's intention is that we be conformed to the image of his Son. Imagine responding to suffering as Christ did. We might be misrepresented, abused, or physically exhausted. We might be in the crucible, under severe pressure. God's will is that we patiently endure, without bitterness. And that happens through the process of suffering. In other words, rather than explaining away suffering, we ought to realize that things may well get worse before they get better (also a major theme in the book of Revelation). It's not so much that the passage has been twisted, as that it's been only partially understood.

About Predestination

If you board a train whose last stop is where you intend to go, then as long as you stay on the train, you will get to your destination. However, you are not compelled to stay on the train—you can get off at any station. God knows beforehand who will stay on the train, and those he foreknew he predestined "to be conformed to the image of his Son." What is the destination of the train, that is, God's plan? The destination is for us to become more like Jesus Christ, "that he might be the firstborn among many brothers and sisters. And those he predestined, he also called; those he called, he also justified; those he justified, he also glorified."

God brings good from evil, because for those who love him, he works everything together for good. But *how* does everything work together? As it says in verse 29, the plan is for us to become like his Son, like Jesus. Didn't Jesus suffer? Then what makes us think *we* aren't going to suffer? Didn't he pour himself out, giving selflessly to other people? Then, make no mistake, we are bound to experience similar sufferings. God has revealed certain things about himself to us: he is self-sacrificing love; he gives himself to others; he is inviting us to share in his life. That means we, in becoming more godly, will become more self-sacrificing and giving. Do we long to become more godly—in this way?

Self-Sacrifice at Every Life Stage

Life itself schools us in managing suffering. The various stages and relationships of life—if we are to navigate them well and continue to grow in character—will entail considerable suffering. Yet there is no other way. To become more like our Creator, we will sometimes suffer in the process.

All relationships entail suffering. Marriage doesn't work without forgiveness, compromise, and sacrifice. Neither does parenting. Any close friendship is characterized by emotional pain: we will hurt each other. There are people who claim never to have friction or disagreements, but avoidance of real differences is hardly a healthy way to grow in friendship. This process of transformation isn't solely achieved in personal relationships, but for most of us this is the central arena where character is proved—and improved. It's a process (Philippians 3:10–11).

Marriage

We are created to be social, and being in relationship forces us to think about others. Men and women fall in love. For most, marriage is in the cards.[3] We can give people the wrong idea about marriage. We can mislead them with, "Brother, God has a very special sister picked out for you, and your life is going to be just wonderful. Now you won't lust—it will all be taken care of with a God-given outlet. And you'll always have companionship, you'll complement each other, and everything will be so much easier!"

But people need us to tell the truth about marriage. The

apostle Paul said those who marry will have much trouble in this life (1 Corinthians 7:28), and their interests will be divided (7:33–34) because husbands will want to please their wives and wives their husbands—while also seeking to please the Lord. There is sometimes a conflict between the two. Paul made it plain that marriage is hard, yet many of us as single men imagined marriage would be the solution to all our problems. While marriage is wonderful, and a mystery (Ephesians 5), it is also painful. Let's be honest—we can all be hard to please at times. To have a close relationship with anyone requires sacrifice, and that hurts.

And one day—it may be after three decades, or just three months—we wake up next to our spouse and think, "Who *is* this guy (or gal) in bed beside me? I expected *this,* but *now* that happened!" It is often said that men marry women thinking they will never change—but they do. And the woman's mistake? She marries a man believing that he will change—but he doesn't. Yet, in the wise admonition of Thomas à Kempis (1380–1471), "Be not angry that you cannot make others as you wish them to be since you cannot make yourself as you wish to be." It has also been noted that opposites attract, get married, then attack. That can be a whole world of suffering!

Like most couples, my wife and I have had some tough times. First off, it surely cannot be easy being married to me. I'm not only a male, but also a bit pigheaded. I may be knowledgeable when it comes to history or ancient Greek, but I'm not particularly objective in the area of relationships. I have changed *some* since we married (thirty-three years ago), and at this rate, I may be Christlike in 3000 years. But based on the current trajectory, I'm going to keep needing God's grace—all the time. Although we are weak, those of us who marry can easily have a *functional* marriage—perhaps an okay relationship—but without self-sacrifice, we will never have a *great* marriage. To have a great marriage, both partners must deal with their own selfishness.

Child Raising

Next life stage: kids. And they do not contribute to serenity in the home. In the beginning, they do little else besides the three P's—puke, poop, and pee—and they don't even smile often! Then, later, they smile, but you soon discover that you have to give even more of your time and attention to them. This forces us to put ourselves on the back burner. For us men, it is nearly unimaginable what our wives go through: to have a baby living inside for nine months, and then the breastfeeding and the total commitment to being a mother and still a good wife. How do women do it? It is an honorable but draining life. Having children matures men too, as they shoulder the responsibilities of fatherhood. All this dedication to selfless serving causes us to be more like our Creator.

Aging Parent Care

While our kids are growing up, our own parents get old. My father required little care until the final weeks of his life. My mother, on the other hand, suffered (like her mother) from dementia. She passed through all seven stages of Alzheimer's, requiring constant care and monitoring for several years. Most of us will need help once we enter the twilight years.

Our roles may be completely reversed. We become parents to our parents, and we take care of them like children in many ways, often while we are still caring for our own children. Thankfully, in most cultures there is still the expectation to have the decency to look after one's parents. Certainly, Christians will do so, or, the Bible declares, we are worse than unbelievers (1 Timothy 5:8). As this implies, many unbelievers care for their aged parents, while some Christians may not. It can be a stressful, even painful period in our lives, but a rewarding and humbling one as well.

I have a friend, John, who has been a Christian for maybe seventy years. When his mother was old, she had to wear adult diapers, as happens sometimes. In caring for her, he ended up changing his mother's diapers whenever he was with her. Her side of the family were all atheists. She had a few friends, ones that she played bridge with, but they were infrequent visitors. She said to her son one day, "You know, John, my atheist friends would never change my diaper. But you always do." John replied, "Well, I'm a Christian, and that is what Christians do. It's OK; I love you, Mom." It had a powerful and profound impact on her, and that old, atheist woman was baptized and spent the remainder of her years as a Christian. There is something truly incarnational about this kind of service (John 1:14; 13:1–15).

In the incarnation, God entered our world of sin and filth, and through Jesus Christ, he got dirty. During our lives, there are many opportunities for us to become more Christlike, including suffering, serving, learning, and loving; and it is predestined that we will, whether it occurs in the crucible of marriage, while parenting children, or in caring for our parents. Isn't that amazing and wonderful?

Valuing Relationships over Pleasure

We must *change* to experience the joy in serving others. The course of life naturally tends to break us down over time. But in Christ, if we stay close to the Lord, we have a divine motor that will keep us going during this process of becoming more like him, so that we do not experience burnout in making loving sacrifices for others.

> People prefer living in pain to dying, even when they have no qualms about death itself—they simply value life under any condition as of higher worth than avoiding pain. Some people would take pain of any kind and all kinds upon themselves for any duration rather than betray certain convictions—political, moral, religious, or otherwise. And for those people who really know what friendship is, no cost in pain is too great to prevent the loss of a friend. If we know what life totally devoid of any kind of pain was like, we would probably choose life with pain over life without it.[4]

Sacrifice will sometimes tie us down. We all want freedom, but there is no such thing as absolute freedom anyway, just some liberties with different sets of limitations. God's agenda might not be to create a universe that is merely a theme park full of amusements for you and me. Nonetheless, our flesh will often rise up and pout, *"If I were God, I would make all the rides free, there would be no lines at all, the popcorn would be free, and so would everything else!"* Was that God's agenda? Apparently not.

If we are to become like our Creator, we must shake off this obsession with fun. A couple of times I have met Yale theologian Miroslav Volf. This Croatian scholar has an interesting critique of Western culture. He says our culture is really about "the managed pursuit of pleasure." That is an interesting way to put it. It is the pursuit of pleasure, but it is all managed, as in "How can we offer the best experience at our amusement park?" The best experience while you're using *this* computer; while eating in *this* restaurant; while on *this* cruise; the best and most seeker-friendly experience in *this* new church? Or whatever it may be! It's all about entertainment, fascination, and titillation in every possible sense.

God is not obsessed with that, and we must move away from the pursuit of pleasure if we are to go in the direction of resembling our Creator. He does not force us to love him; we have free will. But if we do right in our natural human relationships, loving the brother or sister we can see, then we can love the God that we cannot see (1 John 4:20). There is something profound about this.

Conclusion

So we understand that the Lord can use pain for good. It is

powerful. I love the way C.S. Lewis memorably summed up the value of pain: "God whispers to us in our pleasures, speaks to us in our conscience, but shouts in our pains: it is His megaphone to rouse a deaf world."

RECAP

- Pain serves a useful purpose. It alerts us when we are in danger (physical or social).

- Every stage of life and every relationship entails sacrifice and suffering.

- Romans 8:28 is properly understood along with Romans 8:29. That is, God's plan for our lives entails suffering (Romans 8:17), because that is how our characters are shaped to become capable of true (Christlike) love.

- We please God when we value relationships over pleasure. That means we must reject the world's "managed pursuit of pleasure."

- We are called to pursue holiness, not happiness.

---

1. "The six children come from three families from northern Pakistan. The research team found the children after hearing about a boy who apparently felt no pain. The boy stood on burning coals and stabbed his arms with knives to earn money. He died in a fall before the researchers could meet him. But the team was able to find members of the boy's extended family. They also seemed unable to feel pain. These children were six to fourteen years of age. They sometimes burned themselves with hot liquids or steam. They sat on hot heating devices. They cut their lips with their teeth, but felt no pain. Two of the children bit off one-third of their tongue. Yet they could feel pressure and tell differences between hot and cold… [All] had a gene with a mistake, or fault. Except for the genetic fault, the children had normal intelligence and health. The researchers found that each child received a faulty version of the gene from a parent. The gene is called SCN9A. It gives orders to a protein that serves as a passageway for the chemical sodium. All nerve cells have such passages. This is how pain signals from a wound or injury are communicated to the spinal cord and brain." – From the transcript of the radio broadcast "Scientists Study Children Who Feel No Pain," *Science in the News*, Voice of America, February 2007.

2. https://en.wikipedia.org/wiki/Seven_(1995_film).

3. The Bible does not say that marriage is for everyone—see Matthew 19 and 1 Corinthians 7—only that it's normative. There are exceptions.

4. Willard, *Allure of Gentleness*, 117.

Chapter 7

Is God "Nice"?

It is a dreadful thing to fall into
the hands of the living God.

(Hebrews 10:31)

Oh, the depth of the riches of the wisdom and
knowledge of God!
How unsearchable his judgments,
and his paths beyond tracing out!
"Who has known the mind of the Lord?
Or who has been his counselor?"
"Who has ever given to God,
that God should repay them?"
For from him and through him and for him are all things.
To him be the glory forever! Amen.

(Romans 11:33–36)

The Truth about God's Nature

By this point of reading the book, you have several insights into the reasons for pain and suffering: There is free will in this universe, and we wouldn't want it any other way. Pain and suffering are essential to life—and part of a dangerous world. Suffering of all kinds is necessary to build character, in sports, at work, in our families, and in all other areas. We become humans capable of love when we put others first as we become conformed to the image of Christ (Romans 8:29; 12:1–2; 2 Corinthians 3:17–18; 4:16–18).

But can anyone really boil down the profound subject of pain and suffering to a half dozen simplified points? We may still be left with many "Why?" questions. You may feel like this:

> *Okay, God, I know this is helping me become more like you, and I understand, I get it—I've got free will, and yes, most of my suffering is self-inflicted. But Lord, there are billions on the planet who don't know you. I look at the standard of life in so much of the world, and I wonder, Lord, will not the Judge of all the earth do right?*

Did you think we settled everything in our examination of Abraham's "negotiation" with God about Sodom and Gomorrah? Who knows but that in a few years Abraham was grappling with the justice of God once more, perhaps when he was asked to sacrifice his son (Genesis 22). A thoughtful human, and especially one who takes Scripture seriously, will continue to wrestle with these issues. I would say this is part of a genuine, lifelong pursuit of God's justice.

The goal of this chapter is to make an important qualification—to urge a certain realism, along with an acceptance of the world as it truly is. I don't mean that we should settle for the values of the world. What I do mean is that we who are believers need to live in the real world:

- We shouldn't pretend that all problems are easily solved.

- Nor should we act as though the stakes are not high or there is no reason for concern.

- Neither should we offer simplistic answers. As in the case of Job, a full explanation may not be offered anytime soon.[1]

Telling the Truth about God

Just as we need to tell the whole truth about marriage (as we discussed in the previous chapter), we need to tell the whole truth about God. He is willing to let people suffer, without immediate intervention. How many hours was Abraham agonizing over God's command to give up Isaac?[2] How many years (decades? centuries?) did the Hebrew slaves call out to Yahweh for forgiveness before Moses was ready to challenge Pharaoh?

Consider Joseph. He is thrown into prison, first having been sold into slavery by his jealous brothers. *Twenty-two years later,* his take on it is: "Don't blame yourselves; it was God's will. Now I am the number two guy in Egypt, and the Jews don't have to starve. (This was a time of great famine.) There's food here, so let's move the whole family to Egypt, where they can survive." (Of course, generations of Jews would later be enslaved, but Joseph did not know that part.)

It turns out well for Joseph, but it is not exactly smooth sailing! After he is sold by his brothers into bondage, a traumatic event, he wins favor in his master's house. Joseph is respected as a responsible and trustworthy servant. ("The cream rises to the top.") Yet soon he is falsely accused in a sexual scandal. Charged with misusing his position, he is flung into jail. He interprets the dreams of the baker and the cupbearer, and one of them remembers him—but a little too late. He languishes in jail for two years more.[3]

A few days ago I led a communion service in the Garden of Gethsemane, where Jesus, betrayed, was delivered over to the security forces of a corrupt high priest. Jesus had to go through the agony (Luke 22), but he knew the resurrection would follow. As you read the Gethsemane story, does it seem to you that Jesus took great comfort in knowing he would rise from the dead? To me, it seems his personal horizon is filled with storm clouds. Sweating heavily under the pressure, Jesus implores God to rescue him, and he identifies with the psalmist in Psalm 22, a psalm whose flow moves from a sense of dereliction to confident expectation of rescue.

Yahweh is the God who is willing to let us suffer, yet sometimes we are obsessed with showing our friends that God is "nice" and that he wants us to be nice people. That is what Christians are: they are nice, and we need to have a nice church, right? But there is *nothing* in the Bible about God being nice.

That is not one of the words that describe him. ("Merciful," "loving," "patient," and many other words fit, but not "nice.")

Horror

I was shocked to hear about human sacrifice the first time I visited the East African nation of Uganda. But I kept reading about it in the newspapers, and the next time I went there, it seemed that the problem had worsened. Human sacrifice!— just as among the Canaanites, or in the New World, among the Aztecs and Mayans; among the Teutonic peoples of Europe; or in the South Pacific. Just about every place in the world has had human sacrifice. It might not be as common today, but it is rife in Uganda. I divided the Ugandan population into the US population to calculate a comparable figure. I computed that every week, in the United States there would be 100 children who went missing—decapitated, their bodies chopped up for use in witchcraft.[4]

Uganda came to the center stage of current events in the 1970s while suffering unspeakable horrors during the reign of military dictator Idi Amin. Torture and murder were committed on a grand scale. The so-called King of Scotland,[5] Idi Amin (1971–1979), killed between three hundred and five hundred thousand of his enemies, often just because they were from the wrong tribe. When I was there, they asked me if I would like to see the torture chambers of Idi Amin. "It's not a tourist place, but we can get you there." It is an underground chamber. The lower level was filled with water. Amin's soldiers would entice the prisoners to run through this wet zone, telling them they were free to go. But when they entered the water, the soldiers would connect electrodes and electrocute them. The rest starved to death. No one escaped. I saw handprints all over the walls of the various torture chambers. I knew the answer before I asked the question: "How did they smudge their handprints onto the walls of the chamber?" With their own blood and excrement.

To this day in the region, children are kidnapped and made into killers. I have read the history books and spoken to the survivors, and contrary to my expectation I have found strong men and women who are ready to move on. Many have kept their faith, refusing to retaliate or take up the sword. Their strong, buoyant, and forgiving spirit is astounding.

I've ministered in a number of African nations recovering from civil wars. I've met men and women who have witnessed executions, lost all their property, or even endured the killing of family members. They do not necessarily conclude that God has abandoned them or that he doesn't exist. They have another way of seeing things. In fact, in many of the countries where I have taught—like Romania, Vietnam, Peru, Lebanon, Rwanda, Sierra Leone, and the Ukraine—I've been overwhelmed by the resiliency, faith, and willingness to process the past and move on.

On a recent trip to Israel I passed several sobering hours in Yad Vashem. This is a huge campus, an indoor-outdoor Holocaust memorial and museum. A few years ago, I had dinner with a survivor of the Holocaust. Like World War II veterans, they are fast dying out. And yet it was not all that long ago that Hitler orchestrated the deaths of six million Jews, as well as instigating medical experiments on people with varying physical and mental challenges. Millions more gypsies, Slavs, and homosexuals were rounded up. Some thirteen million people died.

I have visited Cambodia several times, and walked through the Killing Fields of the 1970s. They were inspired by the Maoist agrarian revolution of China (1967–1976), in which all the engineers, teachers, and other intellectuals were sent to work in the fields—except that they went even further in Cambodia. During Pol Pot's regime it was decided that anyone who was educated—say, those who spoke French or English—should be executed. The Khmer Rouge effectively decapitated their own country. All the leaders and the thinkers were killed, with almost no exception. I think five doctors remained in the whole country at the end of this "revolution." It is incredibly painful to contemplate.[6]

They thought they were leading a scientific Maoist revolution, so when someone went to the prison they recorded their information, and when they were executed, they took their photograph. There are walls and walls and walls of these photos. The most striking image for me was of a man who looked about the same age I was when I was baptized at eighteen. I used to think that was old and wished I had been baptized at sixteen. Now I am thinking eighteen was pretty early. On his photograph was written "23/10/1977." The thought haunted me: *That was the day I got baptized.* It was the picture of him right before he was executed. In a way that was my first day of life, but it was the day of the end of his hope, his last day on earth.

In most of the Killing Fields, they buried hundreds or thousands in mass graves. In one grave were four hundred people who had been bludgeoned to death. In one, forty-five beheaded children. In another, seventy-five bodies of women shot. If you ever go there, you can still see bits of bone, teeth, and clothes. Two million people out of the seven million in the country died! But there have been other genocides, in Rwanda, Armenia, and many more countries.

In many action movies, the North Koreans really come out bad. But we should not equate the government with the people, who deserve guidance and support, not the harsh regime that has been in place for so many decades. North Korea, like the former Soviet Union, has a *gulag*, where they send anyone who rejects the cult of communism (and emperor worship—not so different to ancient Roman times). Their *gulag* contains 150,000 prisoners. Up to half are there because of their faith, as honoring any god above their dictator is a crime. It is estimated that as many as 70,000 believers in Christ are imprisoned in North Korea.[7]

People are executed every week rather than give up their faith. Adherents of other religions face imprisonment and death, but it is overwhelmingly people who believe in Jesus Christ who are jailed and executed. Where faith is illegal or repressed, some governments have gangs that prowl the cities, roving from house to house looking for Christians and dragging them to prison, just as the apostle Paul did when he was the persecutor Saul of Tarsus. This still happens today, for example in Egypt and Iraq. Christians are hunted down and executed.

A World Gone Mad

Although none of this is God's doing, one might say that everything described above happened on God's watch. God causes everything or permits everything, and many of us reflect on what kind of a god lets that go on. If you were God, wouldn't you have stopped it? I am not charging God with wrongdoing; I am merely saying that this is hard to figure out. Every year when I visit somewhere, talk to survivors, read a news report, or watch a documentary, it seems like the whole world has gone mad, totally inhumanly insane in the way we treat each other. Butchery, trafficking, and slavery are still alive and well. *And God allows this.*

This is not primarily about intellectual answers; it's about wrestling with the heart. Easily one third of the psalms feature a simmering resentment toward God. Psalms of lament, of mourning—psalms of disorientation, as one Old Testament scholar calls them. Things are not good; these psalms do not express happiness. That is why I think the psalms relate to so many people, and we relate to them. One year on my website, I started forty days of quiet times with ten from Psalms—topics like the darkness, psalms of sin and confession, the psalms and hymns that we should never pray.[8]

An Answer—But Not an Easy One

God is certainly able to remove pain and suffering from the world—so why doesn't he? Because he wants *us* to do that! That is where this has been leading. Our goal is not just to be law-abiding church members in good standing; we have got to do something about what is going on in this world. Not just, "I'm going to give ten dollars more to my missions contribution this year. You've prodded me; my conscience is pricked." It's bigger than that.

I mentioned before about God not being "nice," and that may have made you feel uncomfortable. God has compassion, goodness, and mercy; he is perfect, pure, just, and holy, but never once is he said to be nice. God will upset you; he will bother you. If you are seeking the Lord, and you are not a Christian, know that he is going to mess up your life—severely. You are not going to get to do some things you wanted to do. Some might think that this kind of honest reflection about God could drive seekers away. More likely they will walk away from the discussion thinking, "You know, those believers don't mince words—they seem more concerned with the truth than with sugar-coating everything or explaining it away."

God will give us the grace we need to stand up under trials, but it is not easy. It has to do with the cross. God is not "nice," which means our goal is not to be nice, although we should be relatable and easy to be with. We need to be compassionate and caring toward others, but if our goal is to not upset people, for people to like us, and to be politically correct, we will never follow Jesus for long. The goal is not to establish a nice church. It is nothing like that; he is going to bother us and, sometimes, we will bother people.

God is awful (awe-ful), in the sense of inspiring awe; he is also terrible. Terror is a profound, bone-chilling fear. There is something about the presence of God. In both Testaments, sometimes people come into his presence. You may think they must be all smiles and butterflies. No, people turn pale as the blood drains from their cheeks, they fall to the ground, they can't talk, they can hardly even move—they are utterly terrified in the presence of God. He is not our cosmic buddy, he is a consuming fire. *And* he loves us, so try to process those two things: his incinerating holiness, and his all-embracing love to the point that he sent his Son to die for us. And we are supposed to believe that both those things are true!

It is just like believing in hell, *and* we are always to rejoice. How do you do those at the same time? This realization that God is not nice is part of a full-orbed faith, so we are not left flapping in the breeze when hard times come. But many Christians are at a loss when troubles come, because someone told them, "Oh, life will be easier; become a Christian and you'll see." True, life is easier in some ways. The self-inflicted pain goes down, but the world will still beat you up. There will be persecution. You will be part of a wonderful family that will accept you, but you will not, if you want to live a righteous life, escape opposition.

God is not nice—take that away from this chapter. Put the book down now if you need to, and think about that. And then read on.

Simplistic Diagnoses

Many people have said that God is punishing gays by sending AIDS, including many religious leaders. Of course, the problem with that is that most of the people who have AIDS are not homosexual. So, those who say, "Mark my words, that was

God!" are slandering God and misrepresenting the Scriptures. Why did so many people die in the 2010 earthquake in Haiti? Lousy government within, tampering without, but when someone says people died because of God's punishment for voodoo, they are completely, hopelessly wrong.

But we like these kinds of uncomplicated answers. When Job suffered, his friends said, "You must be sinning!" Actually, Job agreed in principle; he had the same theology as they—he believed that God disturbs us when we sin. "But I didn't sin, so why is this happening?" Job did not understand that God sometimes disturbs us even when we have not sinned. He held the same view as Eliphaz, Bildad, and Zophar, except that Job knew he didn't do anything wrong. Sometimes God lets a person suffer, or even go to prison, who has done nothing to deserve it!

Remember the blind man of John 9? His disciples asked Jesus, "Who sinned, this man or his parents, that he was born blind?" They didn't really see this poor soul as a person; to them, he was a cipher—in a sense, a nobody, a theological quandary. Jesus challenges them. He says, in effect, "You're asking the wrong question." He reminds them that this situation exists so that God may be glorified. Indeed, the glory of God was revealed in this situation. When we speak about (or to) people in difficult or painful circumstances, we need to take care not to grab for easy answers or simplistic solutions to serious issues. Otherwise, we run the risk of appearing insensitive, naïve, and even perhaps harsh.

I have heard from some well-meaning Christians, basing their ideas on Isaiah 57:1, "the righteous are taken away to be spared from evil," that God takes away the innocent, the righteous, so they won't suffer more. They mistakenly believe that if someone is killed in an accident, it is always because God knew that something worse would have happened otherwise. That would mean that, for every highway death, we can be sure that God was just whisking someone away so they would be spared from something else. We simply cannot know that.

Similar statements are, "God always protects true believers" and "It's better that way." Doling out such saccharine pronouncements is like a doctor slapping an adhesive bandage on a deep wound (Jeremiah 6:13–14). It does little to cure the soul.

RECAP

- God is merciful, loving, patient, and many other things, but he is not "nice."

- God allows sometimes unfathomable degrees of oppression and pain. He does not necessarily intervene, and when he does, the intervention isn't always quick. Men and women of faith ought to be in touch with this aspect of the real world.

- We shouldn't act as though the world's problems can be easily solved.

- Nor should we offer simplistic answers.

1. And perhaps never at all. While every tear will be wiped away, there is no biblical promise that every question will be answered.

2. God did show by this that he disapproved of human sacrifice—that is one of the points of the story, because back then people sacrificed their first-born child. But even though Abraham knew that Isaac would be spared in the end, he truly believed that his son was going to die. We cannot oversimplify the situation by saying it turned out well, because this was a father willing to kill his beloved son. Yes, he reasoned that Isaac would be resurrected—the New Testament tells us that—but he also believed he would have to go through with the act of killing him! And worse, his God nearly allowed him to do it. What is the difference emotionally between that and actually carrying it out? Abraham had the knife in his hand, ready to plunge it into his own boy.

3. And Paul, while imprisoned, preaches the truth to Felix (Acts 24), but Felix has a different agenda. He is hoping for a bribe, so he leaves Paul in jail two extra years. But two years, or twenty-two years—it's a long ordeal either way.

4. In Uganda I asked my hosts what I should speak on during the Sunday service, and they said they wanted me to speak about witchcraft. Why witchcraft? Because everyone there is affected, and because human sacrifice is so big. The witch doctor says, "We'll need a liver for this"; "If things are going to go well and you want blessings, we'll need two kidneys for this"; or "So, you're launching a new company, starting a new enterprise. This will require a human sacrifice. We'll behead a child."

5. *The Last King of Scotland* is a novel by journalist Giles Foden. Focusing on the rise of Ugandan president Idi Amin and his reign as dictator from 1971 to 1979, it is written as the memoir of a fictional Scottish doctor in Amin's employ and interweaves fiction and historical fact. The film version was released in 2006.

6. And Pol Pot had been a school teacher! Chao Ponhea Yat High School was taken over by his forces and turned into Tuol Sleng, the infamous S-21 prison camp, where people were detained and tortured. Every room

featured creative ways of torturing people. They had metal beds onto which people were attached to be tortured until they confessed—they were innocent, of course. What happened there was captured in paint, because there was an artist among the prisoners. In this prison, there were over seventeen thousand inmates, yet by the time the Vietnamese "liberated" Phnom Penh, only eight or nine persons still lived. All the others had been tortured and executed, their bodies dumped in the killing fields fifteen kilometers (nine miles) away, where the Khmer Rouge marched prisoners from Tuol Sleng to be murdered and buried in shallow pits. The artist painted pictures of people being waterboarded and tortured with electricity. Some of it was just pure sadism. There are pictures of the guards playing "toss the baby": they would put a baby at the end of a bayonet and they would toss it and catch it, like catching a bale of hay on a pitchfork.

7.   Open Doors places North Korea as No. 1 on its list of the worst persecutors of Christians in the world. See https://www.google.com/search?client =safari&rls=en&q=open+doors+persecution&ie=UTF-8&oe=UTF-8. The USA has over two million in prison, and is leading the world in incarceration. But North Korea is a small country. One reason the number is so big is because in North Korea, they imprison three generations. In other words, your crime is going to affect your parents; you may get them imprisoned for your faith, along with you and your children. It is reported that a huge number remain in prison because they will not give up their faith in Christ. Now, I am just pointing this out—I am not here to discuss their theology, whether they are technically true Christians or understand the New Testament in every correct way. I am sure *I* don't understand it in every correct way; I'm working on it.

8.   There are a few passages in Psalms that, as Christians, I don't think we can pray, such as in Psalm 58. For ten podcasts on Psalms, see www.douglas-jacoby.com.

Chapter 8

The Current of Suffering

What do people get for all the toil and anxious striving with which they labor under the sun? All their days their work is grief and pain; even at night their minds do not rest. This too is meaningless.

(Ecclesiastes 2:22–23)

Blessed is the one who perseveres under trial because, having stood the test, that person will receive the crown of life that the Lord has promised to those who love him.

(James 1:12)

Given the significant degree of pain, harm, suffering, and evil in the world, it would be surprising if God's revelation to humans didn't touch on this reality frequently. In fact, the Bible does address the topic of suffering, directly and indirectly. So many books in the Bible speak of hardship, injustice, and pain, one could say there is a current of suffering that courses through Scripture, from Genesis to Revelation.

Genesis—Decades. In the narratives of Genesis, suffering often endures for decades. In fact, the longer I have been a Christian, the more I have come to view the decade as a fundamental unit of time. We tend to count our time as Christians by months: "I fasted for a month," or "I tried this new prayer plan for six months, or forty days." With the Lord, centuries and millennia are fleeting. In our lives as we attempt to follow God, decades elapse:

- Joseph spends twenty-two years separated from his family, much of the time in prison, before they are reunited in Egypt.

- Jacob leaves his father and goes to Laban. He does not come back and reconcile with his brother Esau until some twenty years later, and by then his mother is dead—the one who was afraid she would lose her son Jacob; and she did lose him because of her meddling.

- Isaac marries Rebekah when he is forty. They had never met each other; Isaac's father, Abraham, had delegated it to a servant to go to the old country and get a wife for his son (Genesis 24). By the time the servant gets back, Abraham is apparently no longer alive. (Don't get confused because the first section of Genesis 25 does not chronologically follow Genesis 24.) Rebekah is barren, but in answer to prayer, when Isaac is sixty, the twins are born. They had been trying to have kids for twenty years—two decades of waiting for a prayer to be answered.

- Similarly, Jesus figures out he is God's Son in some unique way when he is twelve (Luke 2). When does he begin his public ministry? Almost exactly twenty years later.[1]

So, for God to make us wait decades is nothing. Older Christians, do you agree with that? Is it really about years, or is it about decades? I propose that the decade is the fundamental unit of life in Christ.

Exodus—Deliverance. In this book God's people, small in number, greatly multiply, constituting a potential threat to the Egyptians. They are enslaved, although we do not know for sure when their servitude began. Eventually, through the hand of Moses, they are delivered, probably sometime in the thirteenth century BC.[2] Did they cry out to the Lord as soon as their bondage began, or did their suffering reach an intolerable crescendo?

God cares—eventually the Israelites are delivered from Egypt. But after how many years of slavery? Perhaps hundreds. But he came through! The lesson is that relief may not come until a long time after we have requested it.

Job—Suffering undeserved. This classic work is a story of undeserved suffering. The theology of Job's friends—his "miserable comforters" (16:2) and "worthless physicians" (13:4)—is that justice is maintained in this life, in this world, through a system of rewards and punishments. The guilty suffer, and the righteous prosper. Or, from the reverse angle, those who suffer must have deserved it, as do those who prosper. Job shares the theology of his friends.

Job refused to give up on God's justice. He would agree with his friend Elihu in Job 34:12 and 37:23: "It is unthinkable that God would do wrong, that the Almighty would pervert justice.… The Almighty is beyond our reach and exalted in power; in his justice and great righteousness, he does not oppress." For men and women of faith, surely this an axiom: God is just; God is good. We start there—and then we try to figure out what is going on.

What does God say to Job? In Job 40:8 he says, "Would you discredit my justice? Would you condemn me to justify yourself?" We must always watch out for our hearts and what our motives may be. I believe the Lord is affirming: "I am in control of the world; I am in control of nature, and so far, I'm doing a good job, so can't you trust me with your life?" He never tells Job about the bet with Satan; he never reveals to him what was really going on, even at the end, when things are a lot better (Job 1:8–12; 42:10–17).

Perhaps putting words into God's mouth, his message to Job might be: "You don't know enough to understand how the world works, Job. As for the problem of human suffering, you aren't smart enough to understand the answer, even if I gave it to you. But you do know *me.* Rely on me." The book of Job reaches its resolution not when he gets everything back, but at the moment when he trusts God.[3]

Psalms—Disorientation. Some forty percent of the Psalms focus on sadness and loss. Mourning, grief, shock, and other emotions are common in this ancient collection of prayers.

Scholars often categorize individual psalms as psalms of orientation (toward God), disorientation (when injustice, abandonment, or oppression are turning our world inside out), and new orientation (after the genuine expression of our pain, working through it and growing in the process). In Psalm 73, the psalmist begins by articulating his deep disorientation, but by the end he has moved to new orientation.

Asaph (c. 800 BC), the composer of Psalm 73 and many other psalms, contemplates relinquishing his faith. In effect, he queries, why am I bothering to follow you?

> *I had nearly lost my foothold.*
> *For I envied the arrogant*
>   *when I saw the prosperity of the wicked.*
>
> *They have no struggles....*
> *They are free from common human burdens....*
> *Their mouths lay claim to heaven,*
>   *and their tongues take possession of the earth....*
> *They say, "How would God know?*
>   *Does the Most High know anything?"*
>
> *This is what the wicked are like—*
>   *always free of care, they go on amassing wealth.*
>
> *Surely in vain I have kept my heart pure....*
> *When I tried to understand all this,*
>   *it troubled me deeply*
> *till I entered the sanctuary of God;*
>   *then I understood their final destiny.*

"They have no struggles"? Not true. "They are free from common human burdens"? Not true either. "Their mouths lay claim to heaven"; yes, and "their tongues take possession of the earth.… They say, 'How would God know? Does the Most High know anything?'" They think that God does not know or care. "This is what the wicked are like—always free of care, they go on amassing wealth." Is this not the American Dream, to be carefree and amass wealth? Some people are actually "living the dream," but most are not. They are suffering in silence, disappointed and increasingly disillusioned. But when we notice the few people who seem to be prospering *without making the effort to follow God,* we can lose our foothold. We may feel, "Surely in vain I have kept my heart pure." "When I tried to understand all this, it troubled me deeply till I entered the sanctuary of God; then I understood their final destiny." With Asaph, we need to take the long view, striving for an eternal perspective.

The Psalms are an excellent source for insight, heartfelt expression, and even prayer. In our church in Atlanta, we give a copy of my book *Thrive! Using Psalms to Help You Flourish*[4] to new members. But I think it's mature Christians who appreciate the Psalms most. They have endured more, seen more, and persevered more.

Isaiah—Suffering Servant. One of the major currents running through this book, especially the latter half (in chapters 40–55) is that of the Suffering Servant. This servant shows up in the four Servant Songs (42:1–4; 49:1–6; 50:4–9; and 52:13–53:12). While many Jewish scholars see the songs as applying to Israel, many Christian interpreters understand these passages to be speaking of the Messiah. But there is no reason to limit the servant's identity, as he may well represent Israel (particularly what the nation should have been) *and* the Messiah.

Recall that in the Old Testament the Messiah is the Lion of the tribe of Judah (Genesis 49:9). But we also read about the Lamb that was slain for our sins, the suffering servant (Isaiah 53:10). With the advantage of our perspective under the new covenant, we understand that these are not two separate persons, but one and the same. In Jesus' day many expected a lion Messiah—a military figure who would eject the Romans and wreak vengeance on all the enemies of God's people. Not so many were waiting for a lamb Messiah! This is the reason many of his own people did not recognize him (John 1:11). In the final book of the New Testament, we read:

> *"Do not weep! See, the Lion of the tribe of Judah, the Root of David, has triumphed. He is able to open the scroll and its seven seals." Then I saw a Lamb, looking as if it had been slain, standing at the center of the throne, encircled by the four living creatures and the elders.*

(Revelation 5:5–6)

While the two images—lion and lamb—are in dynamic tension, they are not necessarily contradictory. In Jesus Christ, we finally apprehend this crucial truth. This perspective can fortify us through our own trials.

Jeremiah—70 years of suffering. Jeremiah 29:11 is a favorite passage and even a pet verse of many, especially in the Health and Wealth movement. "I know the plans I have for you." What exactly are these plans? The main message here is not "He is going to bless you; he has plans for your future." We love verses 11–14, but how about verse 10? Most prosperity preachers skip that one. The Lord's message is, in short, "Settle down in Babylon; you're not going back to the promised land for seventy years. Seventy years of disorientation, of exile among the enemy, away from Zion. You were warned (Deuteronomy 28; Leviticus 26). But you have pushed me to the limit. I do have plans for hope and a future for my people, but it's your grandchildren who may be able to return, not you. Sorry."

And of course many of their grandchildren did make the trek back to the Holy Land—though others preferred the comforts of Babylon. But this happened after the decree of Cyrus the Great, in 538 BC (2 Chronicles 36:22; Isaiah 44:28; 45:1; 45:13). For more on Jeremiah 29 and prosperity theology, please read Appendix B.

Less familiar is Jeremiah's complaint in chapter 12. Like so many of the prophets, he was deeply troubled over the apparent lack of justice in the world. Jeremiah takes God up on the issue:

> You are always righteous, LORD,
>   when I bring a case before you.
> Yet I would speak with you about your justice:
>   Why does the way of the wicked prosper?
>   Why do all the faithless live at ease?

You have planted them, and they have taken root;
*   they grow and bear fruit.*
You are always on their lips
*   but far from their hearts.*

(Jeremiah 12:1–2)

It is true that God always turns out to be right, but why are the faithless living at ease? They are not even trying to please him! Even the great prophet Jeremiah feels like what he is doing is futile. To feel this way is to suffer. The emotional pain may manifest in physical (psychosomatic) pain.

Habakkuk—Where is God? The prophet Habakkuk (c. 605 BC), a contemporary of Jeremiah, is another person deeply disturbed that God's enemies, the Babylonians, are getting away with murder:

How long, LORD, must I call for help,
*   but you do not listen?*
Or cry out to you, "Violence!"
*   but you do not save?*
Why do you make me look at injustice?
*   Why do you tolerate wrongdoing?*
Destruction and violence are before me;
*   there is strife, and conflict abounds.*
Therefore the law is paralyzed,
*   and justice never prevails.*
The wicked hem in the righteous,

so that justice is perverted,

(Habakkuk 1:2–4)

He cries out to the Lord, freely venting his pain and frustration. A large number of great men and women in the Bible express their bewilderment, doubts, fears, or anguish to God. There is nothing wrong with being "real" in this way.

Hebrews—Hanging in there. A dozen times in this letter the Hebrew writer urges us not to quit, not to forfeit our salvation. As examples of saving (persevering) faith, there is the "Hall of Fame of Faith" of Hebrews 11. These individuals are the "great cloud of witnesses"[5] to our own spiritual race.

All these men and women lived by faith, even though at the end they still had not received the object of the promises. They refused to quit. That is real faith—hanging in there even when things are crazy. Even when you are not getting what you prayed for. Anyone can be happy when the weather is fair, but it's about staying faithful for years, for decades, when God seems not to be coming through. He is faithful, and in the end all will be made right—sin punished and virtue rewarded. Hebrews urges patience (6:12).

2 Corinthians—Sacrificial leadership. In this letter, we learn that true leadership is proven by suffering. Paul's authority is being challenged. In this epistle he is simply saying (especially in chapter 11), "I don't want to boast about it, but I have suffered more than you guys have, and that is the thing we should 'boast' about. The mark of true leadership is willingness to suffer." That is his badge, his credential.

In contrast, many modern leaders, like the described "super-apostles" (2 Corinthians 11:5; 12:1) who resisted the apostle Paul, take great pride in their outward appearance (1 Samuel 16:7): looking good, sounding eloquent, possessing fine homes and cars and clothes, and enjoying special perks of ministry. How different from the true apostles of Jesus Christ! (1 Corinthians 4:1–11).

1 Peter—Don't be surprised! This letter is written to strengthen disciples of Christ in a time of high stress or persecution. Nero began to tyrannize Christians in Rome in the summer of AD 64, and his persecution program must have spilled over into the provinces. Sometime in the following four years, both Peter and Paul were executed.

We shouldn't be surprised when we suffer. Peter refers not to the suffering that comes from meddling or murdering, but that which comes from living as a Christian. Pushback and backlash come from our rejection of the world's values. Christ did not lash back: "When they hurled their insults at him, he did not retaliate; when he suffered, he made no threats. Instead, he entrusted himself to him who judges justly" (1 Peter 2:23). This is a hard lesson for us: when he was misrepresented, he showed restraint and love.

Revelation—Peeking behind the veil. The final book of Scripture is Revelation, or the Apocalypse.[6] In apocalyptic literature the curtain is pulled back, allowing us to glimpse heavenly realities. We see that God is in control. Yet a realistic biblical theology isn't naïve. It acknowledges that things may get worse before they get better, and so faith will be tested—and faithfulness ultimately rewarded (Revelation 12:11). Will we still be standing? Will we persevere to the end, or will our love grow cold?

Reality

We have spotlighted eleven books of the Bible. However, the theme of suffering runs all through both testaments. It is more prominent in some books of the Bible than others. Perhaps suffering is such a major theme in Scripture because it is a huge reality in the world. Many countries are poor. And in addition to poverty, there is another set of challenges in scores of nations: religious persecution.[7]

It is not wrong to question God. All the great men and women of the Bible struggle with the twin issues of God's justice and his mercy. They halt, they hesitate. This is drastically different from the cowardly flight from reason and the denial of negative feelings that are common today.

The Cross of Christ

All this should be encouraging, because it's *reality.* God connects with us through Jesus Christ by means of the cross.

- We can't say he does not understand temptation: *"Because he himself suffered when he was tempted, he is able to help those who are being tempted"* (Hebrews 2:18).

- We can't say we had to give in to sin, *"for we do not have a high priest who is unable to sympathize with our weaknesses, but we have one who has been tempted in every way, just as we are—yet he did not sin"* (Hebrews 4:15).

- We can't say that God has not taken pain and suffering into account. Even the crucifixion itself, though launched into action by evil people, was God's plan all along: *"This man was handed over to you by God's deliberate plan and foreknowledge; and you, with the help of wicked men, put him to death by nailing him to the cross"* (Acts 2:23).

And so, let us embrace the cross, not the cushy American Dream. Let us roundly reject prosperity theology, which equates wealth and health with righteousness, because in most of the world such claims are farcical—given global levels of inequality, injustice, and oppression. God calls all of us, through the process of suffering, to become like his Son (Romans 8:29). You could say that he calls us to have a cruciform life, a life that is cross shaped. That is the subject of our final chapter.

RECAP

- Suffering is a fundamental topic in Scripture.

- In many books of the Bible, suffering is a major theme.

- This is appropriate, given the fact that suffering is a reality for all of us. And yet no form of suffering can separate us from the love of Christ (Romans 8:31–39).

1. If he was born in 6 BC, began his ministry around AD 27 or 28, and was crucified in 30 (the year most NT scholars favor), then he was thirty-five at the time of his death.

2. Some conservative OT scholars place the Exodus in the fifteenth century (based on a literal understanding of the 12 x 40 years in 1 Kings 6:1), but the archaeological evidence points more toward the thirteenth.

3. Interestingly, a recent article suggests that at the end, the Lord too repents. The biblical scholar is trying to make sense of Job 42:5–7a, which reads, "I had heard of you by the hearing of the ear / but now my eye sees you / therefore I despise myself / and repent in dust and ashes" (ESV). "After the Lord had spoken these words to Job, the Lord said to Eliphaz the Temanite…" The text seems to indicate that it is the Lord who backs down ("the Lord had spoken these words"). Troy M. Martin, "Concluding the Book of Job and YHWH: Reading Job from the End to the Beginning," in *Journal of Biblical Literature 137, no. 2* (2018): 299–318. Doi: http://dx.doi.org/10.15699/jbl.1372.2018.348082.

4. Douglas Jacoby, *Thrive! Using Psalms to Help You Flourish* (Spring, Texas: IPI, 2014).

5. The cloud of witnesses in Hebrews 12 is metaphorical. There is no biblical evidence that all the departed saints are observing the living.

6. Revelation is derived from the Latin *revelatio*, for disclosure, revelation; *vela* is a veil. "Apocalypse" comes from the Greek *apokalypsis*, also meaning revelation; *kalymma* is a veil.

7. Nations with high levels of persecution: Afghanistan, Algeria, Azerbaijan, Bahrain, Bangladesh, Belarus, Bhutan, Brunei, Burma, Cameroon, Central African Republic, Chad, China, Colombia, the Comoros, Cuba, Djibouti,

Egypt, Eritrea, Ethiopia, Guinea, India , Indonesia, Iran, Iraq, Ivory Coast, Jordan, Kazakhstan, Kyrgyzstan, Laos, Lebanon, Liberia, Libya, Malawi, Maldives, Mali, Mauritania, Morocco, Nepal, Niger, Nigeria, North Korea, Oman, Pakistan, Qatar, Russia, Saudi Arabia, Sierra Leone, Somalia, Sri Lanka, Sudan, Syria, Tajikistan, Tanzania, Tunisia, Turkey, Turkmenistan, Uganda, the United Arab Emirates, Uzbekistan, and Yemen. In other nations there is freedom of faith in much of the country, but there are regions where it is dangerous to be a believer: Ghana, Israel, Kenya, Mexico, and the Philippines.

Chapter 9

Cruciform Life

When Christ calls a man he bids him come and die.
— Dietrich Bonhoeffer

"I die daily" —the Apostle Paul
(1 Corinthians 15:31 NASB)

Less of self, and more of thee...
None of self, and all of thee
—Theodore Monod (1836–1921)

A biblical exploration of suffering and pain inevitably takes us to the cross. Although the cross is a simple (yet profound) key unlocking the mystery of suffering, it still requires explanation. When Christians say the answer to suffering is the cross, the world does not know what that means. And we don't fully understand it either. We need to continue to think about the cross.

Lived by Jesus

As we read the gospel accounts, we take in the depth of Jesus' love, realizing that his cruciform life began long before he went to the cross. The point of this little book isn't to stimulate academic discussion about the problem of suffering, although this is of some value. It is to spur us on to "love and good deeds" (Hebrews 10:24). We best learn how to do this by watching the Lord Jesus in action.

Let's keep our eyes on Jesus. Being conformed to the image of Christ (Romans 12:2; 2 Corinthians 3:18) means we will learn to love as Christ loves. He will teach us. There is no way to this goal apart from suffering. Just as he bore the cross (1 Peter 2:21–23), we too are called to carry a cross. Cruciform (cross-shaped) living is the path of discipleship. The cruciform life is also a kind of crucible; the impurities burned off, the precious gold or silver residue remains. The cruciform life enables us to love with a minimum of self to foul up the relationship.

Lived Out by the Early Church

Jesus not only gave us the Great Commission (Matthew 28:18–20) and the Greatest Commandment (Matthew 22:36–38), but also the charge of Matthew 25:31–45: to care for the sick, the hungry, and those in prison.[1] Christians are supposed to be different.

What were the ancient Christians known for, at least in the first three centuries? (In the fourth century, when the church made a deal with the world, it became increasingly loose and corrupt. From here on, true believers were in the minority of church members.) Christians were known for adopting discarded children. In Ephesus, for instance, where prostitutes worked in the Temple of Artemis, they would take newborn babies that resulted from their "trade" and throw them in the trash heap just outside the city, to die of exposure. Christians would retrieve those babies and raise them as their own. The citizens marveled at this selfless and loving behavior as they witnessed the love of Christ manifested. The Christians were also known for opposing abortion, not by boycotting clinics or the equivalent back then, but by loving all people. They considered all life valuable.

Some were known to bribe their way *into* prisons, so they could spend the night in the cell and minister to the prisoners. They were known for selling themselves into slavery to redeem someone out of slavery. They were known in times of plague not to flee—as the upper classes took flight to their country villas—but to stay in the cities and take care of the dying. When the plague was past, the world remembered that the only ones who cared about them were the Christians.

The early church was radically different from us, counter-cultural, and definitely *not* wrapped up in worldly dreams of wealth and comfort—whereas we are marinated in the juices of materialism. I realize the difficultly of translating such counter-cultural living into daily life. We are not objective, we are deeply enculturated; yet we should still strive for the truth. This is a huge part of what it means to be a Christian.

Living It Out Today

As we grow in understanding, we also need to minister—and not be afraid. We have all been *through* pain, so we can all minister to others *in* pain. You may have lost a loved one, or you may have faced acute or chronic sickness. You may be in pain right now. Regardless, we are all invited to share in ministry.

Open Your Heart, and Open Your Mouth

Rather than remaining silent, consider opening your heart. There is great power in talking about real life issues: death, pain, sickness, separation, divorce, loss, and betrayal—in fact, any tragedy we have lived through. Perhaps you have read William Young's *The Shack.* What is unusual about this book is that usually those who have read it loved it, while those who hated it never finished it—maybe they stopped after only one chapter. Their response is often, "I'm offended! How can God be represented by a woman?" This probably indicates that they never read the book, because when we do, we realize that the author isn't claiming God is female (or male). Rather, in *The Shack* God has temporarily appeared to the protagonist as a woman—since his traumatic father issues prevented him from believing in God as "father."

Any inspiring book, film, or play that helps us deal with the real issues of suffering and pain can touch the heart, plant a seed, and enable us to see who God is with greater lucidity. I am convinced that there are many people who will never become Christians unless we are willing to talk to them about these areas of life that are so hard to bring up.

Talk about the Pain

We are not doing anyone a favor by not talking about real issues. I have learned to talk about the deaths that have affected me. My father died from cancer in 2003, which I wrote about earlier in this book. I could share about my childhood friend, who went to high school with me but skipped his senior year and went to college in 1976, a year before I did. He died of electrocution.[2] My first college roommate, at Duke, died in 1978. When I was baptized into Christ[3] (1977), I didn't know it at the time, but some of the brothers were sharing their faith with Joe. He and I had lots of talks. He said he knew he should put God first, but there were some pleasures he wanted to experience first—and *then* he would be ready to put God ahead of everything else. One night, before we drifted off to sleep, he asked me, "Do you think putting it off a while is okay?" I said, "Well, no, not really. When we put things off like that, we can end up losing motivation."

I will never forget that chilling phone call. It was just before four in the morning when my fellow Duke student Douglas phoned. He said we needed to talk, and that there was bad news. Soon we were standing in the hallway of the dormitory in the dark—I could not even see him; I only heard his voice. "Joe's dead." He had been run over by a train, and they could not even get his body out of the car he was in. I was in shock, but I will tell you this: news like that affects all of us in different ways. Biblically, we should not fear bad news, because we know God is going to be with us (Psalm 112:6–7). Nonetheless, we all react differently. As for me, I was all the more determined to share my faith, because I didn't want anyone else to have to die that way—making vague promises about one day getting serious, but failing to follow through.

Nana (my grandfather's wife) lived until 1980, and I remember her well. I was on a summer term at Oxford when she died. My family did not like talking about death very much; they would try to shield us from it, as I now know. I wanted to fly back to the USA for the funeral, and they said, "No, no, no, don't bother, it's okay." It might have been an inconvenience to them, but for me it would have been a great help (therapeutic) to be at the funeral. Instead, I ended up internalizing the loss.

The same thing happened when my last grandparent died. We were living in Britain, and I was actually about to come back to the United States for a conference. I could have come back one day earlier and made the funeral, but my parents didn't inform me until it was too late. In the family there is a tradition of suppressing what is unpleasant—not talking about it. Are you from that kind of family, one that just doesn't talk about death? Perhaps you may be the one that changes it, in *your* generation. We are not just insulated from death; we are living in denial, and it is not right. Talk about what it's like—talk about how it feels.

My sister died in 1984. I was a student at the University of London. I will never forget that day or that phone call. My dorm had about 500 rooms, none of which had a telephone. There were maybe one or two phones on each floor. (Now everyone has cell phones, but in the 1980s, even making a phone call could be difficult for university students.) The warden (resident assistant, or RA, in the United States) said, "You've got a call." It was my stoic father, emotional and subdued. He said, "Bad news—Suzanne is dead." My twenty-year-old sister. What do you do when you hear news like that?

I held it together; that is what I was trained to do.[4] Yet was this entirely healthy? At my sister's funeral, everyone else seemed composed. The rest of the family had at least had a few days to grieve. I was out of control—crying, weeping, hugging anyone I was near for support.

1984 was a year in which a lot of things changed in my faith and my perspective. When I first started sharing about that, because we just did not talk about it that much in the church, brothers and sisters would come to me and say, "My sister died too," or "I really don't talk about it, but my brother died. I brought it up, and they just changed the subject—but can we talk about that?" It's right, it's therapeutic, it's real.

I have a long list of people I could share about. I wrote earlier about my friend's son, who leaped to his death, and I've known others who have committed suicide. A family member I didn't know well killed himself in 2009, and a friend of the family killed himself, a seventeen-year-old boy that two of our kids used to play with when we lived in Washington. Some in our family have been robbed. Two have been raped. My great-aunt was ninety-nine when a rapist attacked her, tying her up and also robbing her house. Imagine living with the memory of that—till the day of her death at age 105!

The world can be an ugly place. Life is unfair. Suffering is part of our common human experience. Jesus connected with the human condition. He gave us permission to be real, to open up about our pain. We need to talk about the anguish we hold inside.

Value Connection

When my sister died and I flew back to the United States, I was in my hometown of Jacksonville, Florida for the funeral. We had lived in New Jersey (ten miles from New York City) for eleven years, and one of our New Jersey friends flew down. He was a fellow who had tried to study the Bible with my dad. He was fifty; I was twenty-five. He didn't say a lot, but he was supportive. His presence impacted me deeply. It was what I needed.

We lost track of each other through the years, and then he moved, so I didn't see him for a long time, although I saw his wife several times when she came to London on business. Another ten years went by, and finally, we moved to Atlanta. In 2009 I overheard a conversation that prompted me to ask, "Do you know so-and-so?" The fellow said, "Yeah, I know him, and I know what town he lives in." I thought, *I have to go there.*

I called the preacher of the church there to let him know I might be coming into town, and I asked if they wanted to put me to work and just cover the cost of my ticket. He took me up on it, and I spoke to the church. Then I had some unfinished emotional business to take care of.

The great brother who had supported me, and my parents, at my sister's funeral was now seventy-five years old, and I was fifty. I had doubled in age since we'd last seen each other, and now I was the age he was when he ministered to me. But I knew that one of his children had died, and I had not been given the full story. He picked me up at the airport, and as we were driving to his home to have lunch with his wife, I asked him if he would tell me about his son. He quietly lowered his head and said softly, "OK." He pulled the car over to the side of the road.

For the first seven years after his son killed himself, he couldn't talk to anyone about it. But, he confided, over the past two years he had been able to share about the tragedy without completely falling apart. He took ten or fifteen minutes to tell me the story: how his son had been baptized, how he was a great achiever but had a chemical imbalance, and the things he struggled with. And then—it seemed totally out of the blue—he took his life.[5]

After my friend told me the story, and we got to his house, I cheerfully greeted his wife. We sat down to a beautiful salad lunch that she had ready on the table, and the first thing he said to his wife was, "Doug knows." That was all he had to say.

I understand why we don't talk about the hard things, but not talking about them deprives us of a significant opportunity to emotionally connect with other people. We *need* to be open about the things we've struggled with, not just sickness, pain, and death, but also things like our own spiritual challenges, doubts, and disappointments. We might suppose we should never tell an atheist that we, too, face doubt. Yet in fact, an atheist is *more likely* to believe the gospel if you let them see you as a real person.

What would you think if you were an unbeliever and a Christian came across this way: "I'm such a strong believer that

I have no questions about anything; it all makes perfect sense to me. I have arrived spiritually, so come visit my church, because we've all arrived, and we are in possession of the total, unchanging truth, fully rediscovered since the first century." You'd probably be thinking, *Sure, pull the other one!* We are all soft; we bleed. It was not easy for my friend to talk about his son—I know it hurt him, but that was healing for him. It was also healing for me. We have only seen each other a couple of times since then, but you always remember the people who were there when you were really hurting.[6] I have a friend who reminds me, "Don't trust a Christian who doesn't walk with a limp."

So, let's not "waste" a death; use it to bond with others. Sometimes there is nothing you can say, but just being there is personally affirming (like Job's friends during the first seven days). Whether the person was a Christian or not is beside the point. It is something to share.

Talk about betrayal, any tragedy, any loss. One of the most moving sermons I ever heard was in the Garden of Gethsemane. The theme: betrayal. Few hurts go deeper. These are not sufferings anyone seeks. Although we want to become like Christ, to conform to his image, that does not mean we want to be betrayed and would like to be sold for thirty pieces of silver, to know the Lord. That is more of a second-century attitude. Second-century martyrs would say things like, "Bring on the flames. I long for the wrenching of joints, for the teeth of the dogs; let them rip my flesh."

There is no such morbidity in the New Testament text. Even the cross itself is not explicitly illustrated. We may think that back then they had all witnessed death, but that we need to horrify people with a graphic description of the crucifixion to illustrate the gruesomeness of what our Lord suffered. Maybe—but if anything, I believe the brutality of the crucifixion is underplayed in the Bible. The emphasis in the New Testament is much more on the resurrection of Christ.

Make It a Ministry

Use your empathy with the suffering of others to make a ministry. A few years ago, I was leading a tour in Oxford, England and took a chance on sharing candidly with the local guide about some of my own personal losses. Later, I got this message from her. I had given her a book because I knew she was looking for God and faith. She wrote me this email:

> I was sad to hear that you had lost a sister. I had a terrible bereavement just two years ago. My 22-year-old son, John, committed suicide, and I guess I'm looking to see if your book may help my way. There is certainly *something* helping me through every day. Is it just human endeavor—do you think? Do keep in touch.

Good things can happen. We can and must minister to the suffering in the world. The best way to keep our hearts soft, walking in the steps of our Lord, is to *act*. Don't just talk about suffering, make a ministry of it. Serving others can revolutionize our spiritual lives. Following are some further ideas.

Adopt

It is not the cultural norm to adopt.[7] I have been a spokesman for adoption—a huge believer in it. Orphans are the most vulnerable persons on the planet. As someone said, "You can easily judge the character of a man by how he treats those who can do nothing for him."

There are about 150 million ready to be adopted, and I am not so sure there are not another 150 million on the streets who are not ready to be adopted but should be. If we wealthy people would all adopt, imagine how many of these kids would have a home—perhaps all. Our adopted child is, in a way, the star. Our kids all have amazing stories, but she is just radiant. She knows what life would have been, and she experienced the rescue of becoming a Christian in terms of her own adoption.

Downsize

I am greatly encouraged by my younger brother. He and his wife were empty-nesters like us and they made a huge decision. He had had a great job working with AT&T for twenty-five years, but both he and his wife knew they were choking on the materialism of the United States. They said, "Let's sell our house and our car and move to a poor country." For many years now they have been based in Latin America, helping the needy to find jobs, sharing the gospel and baptizing the lost, ministering to the poor, getting their hands dirty, so to speak. This has inspired many (me included).[8]

Visit Prisons

Although the early Christians may have spent more time visiting their Christian brothers and sisters in prison than outsiders, many have learned the power of prison ministry.

Feed the Homeless

I know many Christians who feed the homeless, volunteering in soup kitchens or bringing sandwiches directly to the down-and-out.

Be Family to the Elderly

An estimated sixty percent of nursing home residents never have visitors. According to the National Center for Health Statistics, more than fifty percent of them have no close relatives, and forty-six percent have no living children. They spend weekends, birthdays, and holidays alone—but they don't have to if the Christians are willing to go to them.

Comfort the Sick and Dying

Long-term illness means hours and days of boredom, trying not to focus on the pain and discomfort, while everyone else goes about their lives. When the sick person is up for a visit, we can share some of our time to read to them, play cards with them, maybe even sing to them.

Visit a Poorer Country

Do you need a vacation? Vacatdren to be exposed." Why? Are you afraid of poverty?

I was teaching about hospitality recently, and I was talking to my wife about how in the United States, we can neglect to invite people into our homes. She reminded me of the time we went to a leper's house. We took our kids with us, and one of my children said, "Daddy, he doesn't have any toes." But even in the home of a leper, they served us tea. They took seriously their responsibility, the duty, of showing hospitality to a guest. That is pretty much universal, but a lot of Christians in wealthy countries, where they can most afford it, are not known for hospitality.

Find your ministry: study the Scriptures afresh, looking for this theme of suffering.

Thought Questions

- Am I moved by the suffering of others? Am I stirred to action, or have I become inured?

- Do I accept responsibility for the suffering I have caused others?

- Am I drawn to people who care about other people?[9] To people who share their faith? If we are drawn to someone who knows the good news but does not share it, that is really scary.

- Does my worldview address the problem of pain and suffering? Some religions just deny the reality of suffering; others accept the minimum level of engagement. Christianity is all about it; it is a hallmark of a true Christian.

- What am I doing to help? (Am I part of the problem or part of the solution?)

- Will I always follow God, even if that means experiencing suffering, injustice, and pain?

So how can I know whether I'm embracing the cruciform life? Sometimes a spiritual inventory sheds light on where we are (2 Corinthians 13:5).

- *Have I been misreading biblical passages on suffering?* The Lord's agenda is our holiness, not our happiness.

- *Do I engage in relationships,* despite the risk of pain and disappointment? Isolation keeps us from conforming to the character of Christ.

- *Do I give of my wealth* even though I might prefer to use it to make my life more comfortable? Most believers live at the same standard of wealth as their neighbors.

- *Do I serve in my local church or house church,* even if I am not entirely happy with how things are run? Staying connected despite differences of viewpoint is a true mark of unity.

- *Do I say no to gluttony and drunkenness?* Or do I eat or drink without caution or wisdom? It's not that food and wine are sinful, but overindulgence is sin. (It was one of the major sins of Sodom and Gomorrah, as we saw in Ezekiel 16:49–50).

- *Do I consider my life worth nothing* compared to knowing

Christ, becoming like him in his death? (Philippians 3:7–10).

Attraction

Besides purifying our own hearts and bringing us closer to our Lord, cruciform living has another big payoff. It attracts the lost to Jesus (John 12:32).

RECAP

- God's plan is that we resemble our Creator (Romans 8:29). This we do by being conformed to the character of Jesus Christ—by living a cross-shaped life. Being like Jesus, in a sense, is the *why* of suffering.

- A cruciform life is one that is engaged with others, willing to suffer, and not fascinated with self and pleasure.

- This is how we can have great relationships, not just with our family and friends, but with complete strangers! It's how we connect.

- Rather than suffer silently, it is both therapeutic and evangelistic to open up about our past and present suffering. In sharing our lives, we share the gospel too. (See, for example, 1 Thessalonians 2:1–13.)

1. The dominant early Christian interpretation of "the least of these brothers and sisters of mine" (Matthew 25:40) was that Jesus referred to fellow Christians. In fact, the original role of the deacon (literally, servant) was to minister to the needy within the Christian community. This meshes well with Paul's teaching in Galatians 6:10. See Alexander Strauch, *Minister of Mercy: The New Testament Deacon* (Colorado Springs, Colorado: Lewis & Roth Publishers, 1992).

2. I remember one day picking up the paper and walking into the house. The front-page headline read "Youth Killed in Boat Works Accident." He had been operating an electric sander, fell into the water, and was immediately electrocuted. If you come to my house, I will show you pictures of Adam and me trick-or-treating together. We'd known each other from age eight.

3. Romans 6:3; Galatians 3:27.

4. That day, I went to a lecture at King's College London. A visiting professor from Duke University was speaking on ancient Judaism. I tried hard to concentrate, writing careful (and neat) notes—which I have to this day. I had a Bible study that night with a Singaporean friend, and I said, "I want you to know that my sister just died. I just found out, and I'm going away tomorrow." He said, "Oh no! We should cancel our study—it's okay." I said, "No. No, let's study." We were studying the cross—it seemed appropriate. He was baptized, and I flew home to Florida the next day.

5. I had seen what it does to a parent to lose a child; I saw how it affected my father and mother when my sister died. In 1984 time stopped for them. My mom was a church member, but emotionally, she never moved beyond 1984—all the way till her death thirty-two years later.

6. After we were reconnected, my friend continued to impact my life. We shared meals at several Bible conferences. Through his influence I was able to teach in the African Christian College (Swaziland). I flew down to Texas for his eightieth birthday celebration. Not surprisingly, there were hundreds at the party—far has been the reach of his impact.

7. Several years back we were in West Africa, teaching on adoption there.

My wife went first, then I went, and then our daughter shared what it is like to be adopted. Many of the audience said, "It's not our culture to legally adopt. We look after our nephews and nieces and grandchildren. We have an informal network." That's good, but that is not what the early Christians did. Even the pagans took care of their own. We pushed hard, against the culture, saying, "You need to be willing to adopt, or there is something wrong." I am not saying that every individual should adopt, but we should be willing to do anything that is in the Bible, and personally caring for orphans is repeatedly found in the Bible.

8. I have visited them in Nicaragua several times. The highlight of my second visit was reading stories to schoolchildren. I read stories like "Jack and the Beanstalk" and "The Big Bad Wolf," all in Spanish. I was there with fifty kids, and even up to ten or twelve years old, they love the stories. For the little kids, ages four and five, I dramatized the stories, reading them in character. The youth retreat was great, and speaking to the church was great, but the school visit was the highlight of my trip. The next day I flew back to Atlanta, and the following morning, I flew into Mexico. I did some consulting and preaching, to fifteen hundred people. It was pretty wild, but still the highlight of that week was reading the stories to those kids. And that only happened because my brother downsized. Am I making you feel uncomfortable? Good! That was the idea.

9. Say you are dating a man. He has big muscles, but he doesn't talk a lot. That's okay; we all have different life experiences. What does matter is, does he care about the pain of others? When you went to see *Les Misérables*, and the whole theater was convulsing in tears (because it is so well done), what about him? He said the show wasn't his cup of tea? You were crying—and he felt nothing? Stop thinking wedding bells and hear the alarm bells. What do you suppose: When your children are sick in the middle of the night, who's going to get up? If you get cancer, do you imagine he is going to stick with you?

Appendixes

The final sections of the book are intended to make us more biblically informed and alert.

- Appendix A contains 25 questions and answers pertaining to suffering and related topics. Most were submitted at my website.

- Appendix B exposes the Health and Wealth movement, an unsound theology that is wholly at odds with the cross.

- Appendix C offers nine great points to make in discussions of the problem of suffering.

Following the appendixes is a short bibliography, so that you can continue to explore this vital topic.

Appendix A
Questions & Answers

This appendix is based on the Q&A section of my website, www.douglasjacoby.com.

Q. How long should we keep praying if God is not answering? How persistent should we be?

A. Although it's hard to quantify this, the Bible does give us some clues. Let me share about two who were persistent in prayer. The first is the persistent widow[1] (Luke 18:1–8). She seeks justice, and won't stop until she is heard.

The second is the apostle Paul. He urges us to "pray continually" (1 Thessalonians 5:17). Perhaps this is more a state of mind (a disposition of the heart) than a series of verbal prayers. Paul alludes to a painful reality in his life, a "thorn" that is causing him much discomfort. (What the thorn is, he never says.) Three times he prayed that the Lord would take it away (2 Corinthians 12:8). Then he ceased praying for this, after the Lord told him that the thorn served a purpose.

So, is persistent praying asking the Lord three times? Thirty times? The Bible doesn't give a concrete number of times or a specific length of time to keep presenting a request.

Q. Is sin directly related to suffering?

A. Directly, *sometimes,* though as a rule the wicked are not struck down by lightning any more than the good guys come in first. Indirectly, *yes,* in that when we sin we are likely to suffer more—and be tempted to make others suffer.

Q. In Genesis 2:9 we read that God put the tree of good and evil in the garden, but you have said that God did not create evil. Can you reconcile these two things?

A. First off, God didn't create the tree of good and evil; he created the tree of *the knowledge* of good and evil, which is different from creating evil. Adam and Eve certainly acquired some knowledge of good and evil. Evil, as we discussed in Chapter 3, is not a thing, but the absence of a thing. In the case of humans, it is the rejection of good, the insistence on self-autonomy, living and acting without respect for the will of God. To be clear, the Lord did not create evil.[2]

Q. How does Satan come into play in our study of suffering?

A. To begin with, the Bible does not portray Satan as the counterbalance to God, as though they were equal and opposite forces, as in Newton's third law of motion: for every action there is an equal and opposite reaction. Satan is not like God. He is not all-knowing (omniscient). And, if I understand the Bible correctly, his presence is localized; he is not everywhere at the same time (omnipresent). He is smart and wily, but he is not that smart. In a way, he's a loser. However, he does seem to have power to make us suffer: Paul calls the thorn in his flesh "a messenger of Satan, to torment me" (2 Corinthians 12:7). I am not sure what that means, except that Satan has the power to hurt us. (See the opening of the book of Job.)

So how much harm is he permitted to inflict? All suffering is either caused by God or permitted by him. I would hesitate to attribute *everything* that displeases us to Satan. "That thunderstorm was from Satan, because it burned down my house." We want to attribute events to God or to the devil, because it is easier to think of everything as black and white. We should be careful doing that, but if we look at the picture of the dragon in Revelation 12, Satan seems hell-bent—if I may use that term—on inflicting pain on anyone he can. Whether a painful situation is from Satan or not, either way God is testing is. It will test our mettle; it will demonstrate the worth of our faith.

Q. Can you explain "rejoicing in suffering"?

A. When Paul writes, "We rejoice in our suffering" (Romans 5:3 ESV), it is not so much that we rejoice *because* of our suffering as that we rejoice *while* we suffer. Consider the way Paul and Silas rejoiced while in prison (Acts 16). In one sense, we rejoice in our suffering if we suffer as Christ did (see Philippians 3:10–11). This is not masochistic; "rejoice" does not mean being happy about the suffering. You can be profoundly unhappy about the suffering and still rejoice. Paul explains in 2 Corinthians 12:10 that he is "well content with" (NASB) suffering of various kinds—but it is because he is dependent on Christ's power to bring him through it. Again, he is content *in spite of* undergoing these things, not because of them.

Q. A lot of people I know are on painkillers. Given the role that suffering plays in developing character and a cruciform life, shouldn't we avoid taking pills?

A. There are always dangers associated with painkillers, so yes, I think we need to be careful. Some have potent side effects.

Others are highly addictive. The Lord invites us to share in his suffering (Philippians 3:10; Colossians 1:24), and if we are numb to all pain it's a short step to being numb to the suffering of others. I know disciples of Christ who as a matter of principle avoid all medication, and I respect them for that.

On the other hand, we can't exactly forbid analgesics. In fact, Proverbs 31:6 reads, "Give strong drink to the one who is perishing, and wine to those in bitter distress" (ESV). Relying on doctors and medicine isn't wrong; it's the failure to depend on the Lord that is wrong.

I should probably take advantage of this moment to share my own experience with painkillers. At a difficult time in my life I began to take strong medicine. At first I thought the physical pain was simply from internalizing emotional pain. But the doctors suggested it stemmed from a couple of bulging discs, and from my height. (Tall people are more subject to back issues.) I accepted their advice and began taking opioid painkillers. That was in 2009. The dosages increased, and soon I felt absolutely horrible unless I'd taken my Tramadol. Later, we added a Fentanyl patch, at higher and higher strengths. When I mentioned this to a physician in our congregation, he was alarmed. "That's some pretty powerful medicine, Douglas. You need to be careful." Those words registered, and I determined to reject any upping of the meds. Within a year I had managed to come off the patch. And a couple of years later, I was off the Tramadol. I came off gradually, and this was not easy.

So, from 2009 to 2017 I was on strong painkillers. These days I often read of an epidemic of opioid addiction. Fentanyl is fifty times stronger than heroin. Though I have never used "recreational" drugs, even marijuana, I have more understanding now of the power of addiction. It is easier to imagine myself as an addict. It's easy to get hooked, hard to come down off a drug dependency.

It's better, if possible, to deal with pain through proper diet and exercise. Further, understanding that many maladies stem from unresolved emotional or spiritual issues, we should understand that prayer, genuine friendships, confession of sin, worship, meditating on the Word, and other healthy practices are likely to reduce (or completely eliminate) unnecessary physical pain in our lives.

Q. Can you explain "longsuffering"?

A. An archaic English word meaning patience, "longsuffering" means a willingness to endure for a long time. In the course of our human lives, as I have suggested, such endurance is well measured in decades. Longsuffering isn't just for twenty minutes, but for twenty years.

Q. Some Jewish martyrs were willing to be tortured for a "better resurrection." What does that refer to?

A. This reference, in Hebrews 11:35, is to 2 Maccabees 7, which is about a woman and her seven sons who refused to be released, but embraced torture so that they could gain a better resurrection. I do not know if "an even better resurrection" means more reward in heaven, or that the resurrection of the righteous is better than being resurrected if you are unrighteous. You can take that either way.

The concept of rewards in heaven is biblical. But isn't

heaven the reward, you may ask? Yes, but Jesus also speaks of storing up *treasures* in heaven (Matthew 6:19–21). I think we can go too far with this, but it could be that, as with everything else, the more you put in, the more you get out. Think of it this way. We can both attend the same party, and both of us might have a good time. But you are having a blast while I am merely smiling, because you are wired differently, and so have a different experience of it than I do. Maybe this is because you are the organizer of the party, or because you invited so many people. Others attend the same party, but their level of joy is not the same. So, levels of heaven, or treasures in heaven, could refer to our experience there, as opposed to getting a better stateroom on the heavenly cruise.[3]

Q. If a person with mental illness commits suicide, can God have mercy on them?

A. First, it is not ours to say. The Lord is the Righteous Judge (2 Timothy 4:8). Some Christians believe that if you kill yourself there is no forgiveness possible. While I certainly don't believe in *automatic* salvation for those who kill themselves, the Bible doesn't give us much information about this. There are seven suicides in Scripture, and to abstract a theology of suicide from these is difficult.

In my current thinking, if we are talking about a Christian, forgiveness may be possible. Christians can become unstable mentally (like anyone else) and take their lives. I would be surprised if the Lord did not receive these poor, confused souls with mercy. It should never be suggested that a mentally ill person is no longer in Christ every time an episode strikes.

I used to travel frequently to Ireland. One time I asked, "How's so-and-so doing?" They said, "You haven't heard? He took his life." This Christian brother had a chemical imbalance, and he felt things profoundly. His condition was severe enough that he could not drive. Members of his family pushed him to have brain surgery, which would deal with his emotional swings—but the side effect was that he might not feel anything (his emotions flattened out). He let himself be pushed into getting the operation, but afterward he could no longer experience the joy, or even the sadness, that he had known before. He felt like he was not doing well spiritually since he couldn't "feel" God anymore. As a result, he became convinced that he had committed the unforgivable sin. (He was almost certainly wrong about that.) He went to a park to hang himself but was stopped before he succeeded. Sadly, they let him out of the hospital three weeks later, and the second time, he succeeded in taking his life.

Did he commit suicide because he was rejecting God—being selfish? Or to put it a different way, to what extent does distorted thinking exonerate us from the responsibility to be giving toward others? We probably know it is going to hurt other people if we take our life. But don't we all think differently when in extreme pain or extreme despondency? That is why I do not think we can answer this question decisively. I cannot say that there is no hope for this brother. On the other hand, I don't want to seem to be giving my blessing to suicide as a viable solution. God is gracious, but that does not mean we may act with impunity. It means God is the one who decides.[4] Our part is to be there to offer support, because when it comes to mental illness, much depends on the willingness of others to get involved. (That is why I applaud those who serve as Christian psychiatrists and psychologists.)

Q. Why don't Christians talk more about human trafficking?

A. I have talked with some people who are active in combatting human trafficking, but many churches are more focused on local needs than on stepping out and tackling the problems of the world. We are unlikely to be pricked into action unless we are reminded of the networks of trafficking and slavery—and also because we are overwhelmed by life. In a recent Athens Institute[5] course, we devoted one class session to trafficking. At this time I learned that Atlanta is a major trafficking hub—and this is where I live.

However, we must not mistake the gospel for the social gospel; they are not the same. The church's primary role is not to reverse slavery, nor was it in the first century. The abolition of slavery is a natural result when those in power are affected by Christian ideals. This is not to discourage anyone from becoming involved in combatting this great evil. There are many macro-evils in our world. But it's at the microlevel that we are *all* called to have an impact, sharing the gospel and our lives with individuals (1 Thessalonians 2:8).

Q. Is it wrong to eat animals? Don't they feel pain? After all, in the beginning, God gave mankind plant food to eat. Corn, carrots, and other plant foods do not have a nervous system and feel pain like animals do. I think there is a big difference between vegetables and plant-based foods and animals.

That's why I believe God intended us to be vegetarians. There are also many health benefits to eating a vegetarian diet. It was not until after the Flood that God said it was okay for man to eat the animals. Obviously from the Scriptures it is not sin for mankind to eat animals, but it still seems wrong.

A. Even though the Lord may have intended us to be vegetarians in the beginning,[6] it is far from certain that this is his will for mankind now. Here are a few reasons:

- Jesus declared all foods clean (Mark 7:19).

- Jesus himself cooked and ate fish (John 21:9; Luke 24:43).

- In the story of Adam and Eve, the Lord is the one who clothed the couple with the skins of (obviously dead) animals (Genesis 3:21).

- It would be odd if in his vision the Lord told Peter, "Get up, Peter. Kill and eat" (Acts 10:13) if eating animals is wrong.

- We are to avoid being led away by strange teachings, including doctrines about what we may eat (Hebrews 13:9; 1 Timothy 4:4).

- Christians are not obligated to follow rules concerning food or drink, no matter how well intended or seemingly wise these regulations may be (Colossians 2:16, 20–23).

I am not denying the health benefits of eating lots of vegetables, avoiding large portions of red meat, etc. Yet this is an area of freedom for Christians, and we must respect each other's decisions. In short, if our Lord wasn't a vegetarian, then no one has the right to tell you and me we must give up meat.

Q. Is there a scripture that deals with animal abuse?

A. Proverbs 12:10 comes to mind, though animal abuse is also a violation of the principle of Genesis 1:28. Dominion (ESV), not domination—there is no justification for cruelty.

Q. When disasters happen around our world, what is your response to people who refer to it as an act of God?

A. Insurance companies say, "If it is an act of God, we will not pay anything. If you are killed by lightning, that is an act of God." As we have discussed in this book, everything that happens is caused by God or permitted by God, so I don't think we can always say what is, exactly, an act of God. Rather than trying to figure this out—or worse, playing the "act of God" card as an excuse not to help—our focus should be on the Christian response to disasters. One reason for Christians to avoid frivolous spending and try to save some money is so that they may be able to help others when disaster strikes. We should also get personally involved whenever possible, ministering to victims with our own hands.

Death comes to us all, and so the Lord calls us both to prepare for death and to help others to be prepared. Most people, especially in Western culture, act as though death is unnatural, some sort of surprise—despite humankind's 100% mortality rate. Whether we die "natural deaths" or not, we all need to be ready![7]

Q. If God punishes the wicked in the Old Testament, how can we be sure he is not punishing us today? For example, he could be punishing Haiti for voodoo.

A. In Haiti's 2010 earthquake, we do not know exactly how many people died—perhaps 200,000 or more. I talked to a fellow brother soon after the quake, shortly before I went there myself, and he proclaimed, "I know why the earthquake happened. It's simple." I said, "You mean, because it's a tectonically active region, and volcanically there is a lot going on under there, so that's a place where you're going to have earthquakes?" He said, "Oh no, that's not it. It's voodoo. They sold their soul to the devil, because voodoo is the national religion." (It is said that Haiti is ninety percent Catholic and one hundred percent voodoo.)[8]

Allow me to tell you the reason I rejected the allegation that Haiti's 2010 earthquake was a punishment for voodoo (a popular claim among some preachers). Perhaps voodoo exacerbated the magnitude of the damage, in some indirect way. That is, when people place their hopes in magic or voodoo, they are less likely to work hard or to resist systemic corruption—which tends to reinforce poverty. Sorcery and witchcraft are also used by shamans and voodoo priests to maintain their power, including their ability to profit financially from people's anxiety.

Now if Haiti's destitution is punishment for voodoo, that would suggest that the phenomenal wealth of the United States must have accrued because we who are Americans are righteous. Is the USA a Christian nation founded on Christian principles? Like slavery, expropriating land from the indigenous Americans, and violent revolution? Later, Manifest Destiny was proclaimed, reinforcing the rightness of acquisition of the land "from sea to shining sea." Then the Monroe Doctrine came into play, justifying exclusive influence over the Western

Hemisphere. Were these and other doctrines "blessed" because Americans are (or were) so deserving? No, our accumulation of wealth resulted because we had more guns (and people), not necessarily because we were more righteous.

Q. What about the Prayer of Jabez?

A. A modern author seized upon "the prayer of Jabez" (1 Chronicles 4:9–10) and wrote a major bestseller. The verse reads, "Jabez called upon the God of Israel, saying, 'Oh that you would bless me and enlarge my border, and that your right hand might be with me, and that you would keep me from harm so that it might not bring me pain.'" The book is *The Prayer of Jabez: Breaking through to the Blessed Life.*[9]

In my opinion, this little volume typifies the modern obsession with avoiding pain and striving for comfy living. The fact that God granted Jabez's request (either preventing him from suffering or from inflicting pain, depending on the translation) doesn't entitle us to a cross-free Christianity. God had his reasons for answering that particular prayer as he did. The passage may teach us about God's faithfulness, involvement in our lives, and so on, but it isn't a model prayer. It is misleading to suggest that spiritual people avoid pain, for often the spiritual are given a heavy load to bear. More often than not, we're required to drain the cup of suffering to its dregs (Matthew 26:39).

Note also that there is a translation issue here. It is uncertain whether Jabez prayed that he himself might not suffer pain or that he might not cause *others* pain.

Q. When rape, murder, or other horrible evil happens to a

Christian, how can that person offer comfort to those who do not believe?

A. Sometimes, when we are in the middle of pain or suffering ourselves, we will not be any good at offering anything to anyone. But stay engaged, work at not feeling sorry for yourself, and pursue what the experts recommend: a healthy diet, adequate sleep, steady exercise, and sunlight—those basics can make a huge difference. Above all, you are the one most familiar with your own patterns, and you will know when you are ready to speak about your pain. Like the apostle Paul, who felt unbearable despair, you can come out of it more able to offer comfort than before (2 Corinthians 1:3–4, 8).

Q. Are birth defects a work of Satan?

A. Birth defects happen because of genetic accidents. Both biology and physics reveal a certain degree of randomness in our world. This is not the work of Satan. Yet we must agree with Jesus that such things may happen "so that the works of God might be displayed in him" (John 9:3). This hardly means that God allowed birth defects in order to bring glory to himself, as though he were tinkering with his creations, but it is simply to affirm our faith that even in this God can be glorified. It is an opportunity for grace and for ministry.

Of course, many birth defects are operable; for example, a cleft palate can almost always be repaired successfully. Birth defects may be repaired or not; the Scriptures nowhere say that we are perfectly made. Nor is physical perfection necessary for us to be (or reflect) the image of God. Yet every one of us is "fearfully and wonderfully" made! (Psalm 139).

Q. I have frequently heard Proverbs 22:6 referenced as a promise that godly parenting always leads to godly children. One of my children has rejected God. Is this my fault?

A. Certainly children, the older they grow, have tremendous power to hurt their parents. (I don't ever recall hearing this in a Christian parenting lesson!) In our own family we know both the joy of seeing our children become Christians *and* the bitterness of estrangement. Like all with whom we share the good news, our children have their own will. It's their choice. They may accept Jesus as their Lord, or they may refuse. Even after following him for many years, they can still walk away from the truth. So why is Proverbs 22:6 so misunderstood?

For starters, we like certainty. We prefer absolute promises more than principles whose application may not be so black and white. Next, we tend to mine the Bible for encouraging or interesting passages—like standalone gems. However, many verses are most easily understood when read in the light of other biblical passages, and this is especially true of Proverbs, where a passage may present one facet of a compound truth. (Pardon the frivolity—but what kind of parent was the Lord if his first two children fell from grace? Does this mean he must "step down" from ruling the universe until someone more qualified shows up?)

Further, a single biblical passage may not contain the comprehensive truth on a subject, and this principle definitely applies to the proverbs. The majority are life generalizations—observations about how things usually go. They do not tell us everything we might like to know.

Proverbs 22:6 highlights the correlation between godly

instruction and how our children turn out. Yet this is a generalization, not an ironclad promise. Some excellent parents have rebellious children, just as some children grow up to be outstanding persons despite atrocious parenting. It's not that Proverbs 22:6 isn't true, but it's only part of the truth. To see the entire diamond, we need to step back and appreciate all its facets—not just one.[10]

Q. Does God allow you to have a choice in your pain?

A. The kind of pain we bring on ourselves, yes—at first, anyway. Did Judas Iscariot have a choice? He started out with one, but later crossed the point of no return. Luke 22:3 says, "Then Satan entered Judas." This indicates that we can get to a point where we are broken beyond repair (Proverbs 29:1)—and we have brought it on ourselves. If we go in the wrong direction and make poor choices long enough, there is no hope for us (Hebrews 6:4–6; 10:26–31).

Q. Why does God allow the death of innocent children, as in school shootings?[11]

A. Because we have free will. Killing is something that we do to each other, and *we* can stop these bad things from happening. It isn't God's responsibility, but ours.

If you are thinking that God should take away free will, you must not realize that it would be the end of all of us. You may say that you just want him to stop people from doing bad things—leaving our free will intact—but that is not possible. When you have a wicked thought in your head, should God change it to a thought of something innocuous? He would be playing with our heads—do you think we would still be human?

Q. Our culture keeps us out of touch with real suffering. We in the wealthy West are in a position to effect change in the rest of the world. What is our responsibility as citizens? How do you view Christians' involvement politically, like exerting pressure to stop unethical wars?

A. As Christians, we take our lead from Jesus. He was willing to challenge power, but he did not call his followers to change the world through political processes. In fact, that was not the way of the early church—until they fell in love with the world. Instead, they showed the world an alternate community: the reality of another kingdom, with its own laws and government, a kingdom where the rules are radically different from the rules of this world.

It is not about rights or who's right. It's not about the pursuit of happiness, but the pursuit of holiness. That is what Jesus showed. We need to care, but that does not mean we have to devote our lives to activism. The better question is, what was Jesus' relationship to the power structures at that time? That is an interesting question.

Q. How do we come to grips with the eternal destiny of the multitudes that die because of weather catastrophes like tsunamis, or atrocities like the Holocaust?

A. First of all, we do not decide anyone's eternal destiny. That is up to the Lord. Second, whether we die quickly (as in a tsunami or a murder), or slowly (as with many cancers), it is our responsibility to live righteously and be prepared for death

(Hebrews 9:27). Nor does the Bible speak of a bonus for a violent death. Some questions are posed in ways that are emotionally charged, or carry heavy freight, and that can interfere with our reasoning.

You will go insane if you meditate on hell all day—but we do need to think about it, as it's a biblical doctrine. How I came to terms with the existence of hell is reflected in the paper "Terminal Punishment" (available at www.douglasjacoby.com). Here I examine the various uses of "eternal" in the Bible, and see that it is unlikely Jesus taught infinite torment.

My understanding of the Scriptures—which I have taught since the early 1990s—is that no one will be in hell forever, nor is there infinite torment. Hell is eternal in that is it forever irreversible. All that comes to an end when it should come to an end, depending on what people deserve. Whether it is a million years, five years, or one minute, God is in control of that. So, it is the *fate* of the lost that is eternal.

Let's return to the original form of the question. As someone put it, God has all eternity to listen to the split-second prayer of a pilot of a plane going down in flames. Yahweh is a just Judge, and he does not take pleasure in the death of anyone. (Please read Ezekiel 18:1–32.)

Q. I frequently think about the suffering in this life—more and more with every year—including painful emotional distress. It seems like there is a randomness to life. We read "'He will wipe every tear from their eyes. There will be no more death' or mourning or crying or pain, for the old order of things has passed away" (Rev 21:4). This passage assumes a

divinely determined future order of things, different from the current order, which includes pain, joy, sorrow, happiness, etc. These events may seem random, but all are actually in keeping with the current order God has set up. What do you say?

A. You are onto something important. Indeed the order will change. I believe that in the next life there will be no suffering—and no sin. We will not sin, for the same reason that Jesus did not sin: he saw too clearly what sin was and what it does—he was too smart to sin! In the same way that none of us is tempted to remove our eyes with a grapefruit spoon, so in heaven it would never even enter our minds to violate the will of God.

Strict Calvinists deny the random. We often hear them say, "There are no coincidences," or "Nothing happens by chance." Or they hold that everything has a purpose, ordained by God; he determines what will be, just as he determined what was. He has ordained one person to be saved, the other to go to hell, and there's nothing we can do to affect his will one iota. We rightly reject this view, which makes God a monster. Of course they are right that everything that happens is willed (caused, ordered, or permitted) by God to happen—whether as part of his providential, moral, or permissive will.

Atheists affirm randomness, and see neither meaning nor purpose in suffering—or anything, for that matter. But the world is not meaningless. They give up too easily. Skepticism can be good, but not blindness.

I would say the Lord permits a large degree of randomness. He doesn't interfere with the order of things, with natural processes, or with the consequences of actions. Of course, you and I have experienced his answers to prayer, yet how often does he insert himself into our story to effect a different outcome? Sometimes. If too often, how would anyone detect a miracle? If never, how easy it would be to drift into agnosticism.

At any rate, God doesn't order randomness, if you mean determine its direction—in which case there would be no randomness. But it certainly seems he permits it, from the accidents taking place on a genetic level when cells divide to quantum effects, where determinacy is fuzzy. "Time and chance happen to them all" (Ecclesiastes 9:11).

If the Lord intervened every time someone was about to do the wrong thing, how would we ever learn? If he tilted the playing field every time we were about to score an "own goal," what about everybody else? Rain falls on one farm to bring wet and rot, on another to make crops grow—and maybe on a different type of field to rain out the game. Everyone may be praying for contrary results, so making God directly responsible for all that happens lands us in a hopeless tangle of logical contradictions.

The question has a lot to do with our understanding of prayer. And that's also why I've thought a lot about this. Thanks for bringing up the question.

Q. Isaiah 61 is highly meaningful to me, my wife, and many others who have gone through loss. However, I struggle with the words "instead of," as in "joy instead of mourning." Having lost a child, this is not our experience, nor do I expect it to be in this lifetime. I do have moments of joy, as well as waves of peace. But I don't expect a total replacement... I believe "for" means that God has given me these things as I

focus and battle an emotional wound that I don't expect will fully heal in this life. I suspect I am reading this passage too literally, or that the passage is partially fulfilled in this lifetime and more broadly fulfilled in heaven.

A. Yes, Isaiah 61 is an amazing part of the Bible. All of Isaiah is powerful—no wonder he is the prophet most quoted in the New Testament. Grief—even sustained grief—seems to be part of the human condition, and you are wrestling with powerful emotions, especially as you strive to think theologically and biblically. This is to your credit.

I don't want to read something into the Scriptures that isn't there. And I don't want to overinterpret (or under-interpret) the preposition. Yet I think you're squeezing the text of Isaiah 61:1–4 a little too hard. Here's my take:

- "Oil of gladness instead of mourning"—think how public (and noisy) mourning could be in OT/NT times. Eventually things quiet down, though we may still mourn in our hearts (Ezekiel 24:16–18). Sadness tends to subside, gladness gradually filling the empty spots. (At least that is what we long to experience.) Yet it could be argued that "95% gladness, only 5% mourning" would be a valid instance of the principle here. Just as grief has stages, it also has degrees.

- Consider "bind up the brokenhearted" (v.1). Perhaps the brokenhearted have healed significantly, yet still experience some degree of heartache privately. After all, each heart knows its own bitterness (Proverbs 14:10)—a principle that doesn't seem to be erased in any except the most cheerful (or shallow?) believers. There are things that have broken our hearts too. My wife and I are brokenhearted. Yet we still have the joy of Christ. How can this be?

- Sadness and joy can exist in the same space. Consider Paul's words about suffering in 2 Corinthians 1:3–11.

So if our goal is to reach a place where there is no pain, we may never arrive in this lifetime. On the other side, after the last day has come, and we have been judged and have begun to enjoy our eternal reward, he will wipe the tears away (Isaiah 25:8). The God of all comfort will comfort us. Until then, we live in the overlap of the ages (the present world and the world to come) and frequently experience a mixture of strong emotions. And that's okay.

Q. Why would a God who is omnipresent, omnipotent, and all-loving create people, when he knows such a small percentage will choose to follow him and the rest will be sent to hell?

A. To begin with, it is not wrong to have these kinds of questions. In Genesis 18, Abraham struggled with God's justice in connection with Sodom and Gomorrah. Read the account carefully; the important point is not the percentage of the populace who "made it." The key issue is Abraham's faith in a just God. As he exclaims, "Will not the Judge of all the earth do right?" (Genesis 18:25). A number of other biblical figures shared a similar concern. To ask the question, even the most fundamental bothersome question, is actually therapeutic, and to "stuff" the question may be injurious to your faith. In other words, part of maturing spiritually is being real enough to work through your concerns, even if at the end of the day they are only partly resolved.

Well, why would God create individuals (or allow them to be born) when he knew that they were not going to make it through to heaven at the end? The answer has something to do with free will and something to do with the meaning of goodness. As human beings, we have the ability to make good choices as well as to make bad ones. A moral universe is one where there is right and there is wrong. Moreover, it is possible for beings of free will to embrace good and to embrace evil. If it were not possible for me to do wrong, then why would I be praised as a good person? Goodness is possible for us humans when and only when we have a choice. (Think about it!)

Sure, God could have chosen to create no humans—or no one with free will, which is the same thing. No free will with no risk—but also no people! Bottom line—creating people must have been worth it (and it must be better than the alternative of creating nothing)—otherwise, God, who is always good, wouldn't have done as he did. Interestingly, you rarely hear critics who blame God for the world's injustice suggesting he shouldn't have created *them.*

A final analogy is in order. Why do we choose to have children? Considering the possibility that they might embrace a life of crime, or even turn against us their fathers and mothers, why don't we just play it safe and decide not to procreate? It is worth it for love.

For more Q&As, please visit my website, www.douglasjacoby.com.
You will find more than 1500.

1. For another (historical, not parabolical) persistent widow, see Luke 2:37.

2. Incidentally, the confusion of this fruit with the apple may be due to the similarity of the two words in the Latin translation of the Bible, known as the Vulgate. The Latin word for evil in the name of the tree is *mali* (Genesis 2:17). The word for apples or apple, in other places, is *mala* (Proverbs 25:11) or *malum* (Song of Songs 2:3). Yet in the original Hebrew, the words are not even close. The word in Genesis 2:17 for evil is *ra'*, while the word for apples/apple in Proverbs 25:11 and Song of Songs 2:3 is *tappuach*.

3. For some background on Hebrews 11:35 and 2 Maccabees 7, see the podcast and notes at https://www.douglasjacoby.com/2macc77/.

4. See also Q&A 1367, https://www.douglasjacoby.com/qa-1367-suicide-and-grace/.

5. http://www.athensinstitute.org.

6. The evidence from paleoanthropology does not support vegetarian claims.

7. For more ideas on this topic, see the podcast and notes at https://www.douglasjacoby.com/naturaldisastermp3/.

8. A similar proclamation was issued by David Cho, pastor of the Yoido Full Gospel Church in Seoul (http://english.fgtv.com). He claimed that the Christmas 2004 Asian tsunami was visited upon Japan because of their ungodliness.

9. Bruce Wilkinson, *The Prayer of Jabez: Breaking Through to the Blessed Life* (Sisters, OR: Multnomah Publishers, 2000).

10. For further clarification, please see Douglas and Victoria Jacoby, *Principle-Centered Parenting: Christian Parenting in a Non-Christian World* (Spring, Texas: IPI, 2017). This is the updated version of our original *The Quiver: Christian Parenting in a Non-Christian World* (Spring, Texas: IPI, 2005, 2007). The material on the interpretation of Proverbs 22:6 is the same in all three editions.

11. Two examples are the primary schools at Dunblane, Scotland (1996) and Newton, Connecticut (2012). Sadly, there are dozens more, perhaps most famously the massacre at Columbine High School, in Colorado (1999).

Appendix B
Health & Wealth

Probably the most pervasive, unsound doctrinal system spreading among Christian believers today is the Health and Wealth gospel, also known as Prosperity Theology. I first ran into this theology in the early 1980s, although its roots are in the nineteenth century, and in the twentieth it began to build momentum after World War II.

What do proponents of Health and Wealth teach? Is this completely wrongheaded, or do they make some good points? Once we examine the kernel of truth in prosperity theology, we will examine eight of their favorite passages, and then consider the impact of this movement. We will conclude with a simple challenge for our faith.

This movement teaches:

- God has a plan to bless us physically, spiritually, financially, relationally, medically, etc.

- The degree to which we are blessed indicates our faith and spirituality.

- Pastors and evangelists will become rich if they are righteous, and members too have the same chance to become wealthy.

The biblical emphasis:

- God is good. He does bless.
- He cares about the whole person.
- He is faithful to his promises.

Favored Biblical Texts

We will now take a look at eight pet passages of the Health and Wealth movement. The verses are from the ESV unless otherwise noted.

Jeremiah 29:11–14

For I know the plans I have for you, declares the LORD, plans for welfare and not for evil, to give you a future and a hope. Then you will call upon me and come and pray to me, and I will hear you. You will seek me and find me, when you seek me with all your heart. I will be found by you, declares the LORD, and I will restore your fortunes and gather you from all the nations and all the places where I have driven you, declares the LORD, and I will bring you back to the place from which I sent you into exile.

Context: The passage is normally taken completely out of context. We must guard against the temptation to seek interesting or encouraging groups of words—unless we understand the context and are sure our understanding is right. Verse 10, immediately before this passage, reads, "For thus says the Lord: When seventy years are completed for Babylon, I will visit you, and I will fulfill to you my promise and bring you back to this place." This refers to a period of time two generations *later!*[1]

Covenant: The two covenants are confused. Promises to the Jewish people under the old covenant are not all for Christians under the new covenant.

Deuteronomy 6:10–12

> *"And when the LORD your God brings you into the land that he swore to your fathers, to Abraham, to Isaac, and to Jacob, to give you—with great and good cities that you did not build, and houses full of all good things that you did not fill, and cisterns that you did not dig, and vineyards and olive trees that you did not plant—and when you eat and are full, then take care lest you forget the LORD, who brought you out of the land of Egypt, out of the house of slavery."*

Context: The historical context is the conquest of Canaan.

Covenant: The passage is for the ancient Jews, not the Christians. (We do not take over others' homes and fields in anything corresponding to OT Canaan.)

Implication: This discourages people from discipline and work. Instead, they put their hope in religious acts, sorcery, or giving money to the church—believing that this will make them wealthy.

Matthew 6:33

> *But seek first the kingdom of God and his righteousness, and all these things will be added to you.*

Context: Once again, the promise has been lifted out of context. This promise is only *general* (not all Christians are provided for;

many are poor or languishing in prison). Besides, he speaks of food, drink, and clothing (basic level), not the luxury items of rich Western culture. In fact, Jesus warns repeatedly of the dangers of riches: Luke 6:24; 8:14; 16:14–15; 18:24.

Culture: Prosperity in biblical times did not mean riches and luxury. It meant having:

- enough food to survive
- a good name in the community
- children and grandchildren to carry on the family name

Mark 11:24

Therefore I tell you, whatever you ask in prayer, believe that you have received it, and it will be yours.

Context: Jesus emphasizes our need to forgive others—otherwise our prayers will be ineffective (and our Father in heaven may not forgive us).

Word-faith: This passage is the primary support for "word-faith" theology—which holds that we realize (make real) our dreams by "naming and claiming" them.

Eastern philosophy: This is a mind-over-matter view of how to get things from God.

1 Chronicles 4:10

Jabez called upon the God of Israel, saying, "Oh that you would bless me and enlarge my border, and that your hand might be with me, and that you would keep me from harm so that it might not bring me pain!" And God granted what he asked.

Interpretation: Making avoidance of suffering and unpleasantness such a high priority is contrary to the call to all disciples to carry their cross (Luke 9:23).

Modern bestseller: A modern author seized upon the prayer of Jabez and wrote a major bestseller, *The Prayer of Jabez: Breaking Through to the Blessed Life.* See the comments in the Q&A in Appendix A.

Translation: The English NIV version may even have mistranslated the passage, affecting the understanding of evangelicals like Bruce Wilkinson (who wrote *The Prayer of Jabez*). The original Hebrew may mean that Jabez prayed to be kept from harming others—not to be spared pain himself.

Proverbs 29:18

Where there is no vision, the people perish: but he that keepeth the law, happy is he. KJV

This verse is often misused, claimed as a promise that our dreams will come true. In the Bible, visions came to the prophets, and they preached the Word (Isaiah 1:1; Daniel 2:19; Obadiah 1:1; Micah 3:6; Joel 2:28–29). When Peter cites Joel 2 (Acts 2:17), the context is prophecy. There is nothing here about aspirations, hopes, or a me-directed plan waiting to be discovered.

Translation: The older verbiage of the KJV is misleading, since in the modern West vision is associated with self-confidence, not miraculous revelations. The ESV translates it better: "Where there is no prophetic vision the people cast off restraint, but blessed is he who keeps the law" (Proverbs 29:18 ESV).

Humanistic: The verse is misused to reinforce individualism, and can even lead to narcissism.

John 10:10

> *The thief comes only to steal and kill and destroy. I came that they may have life and have it abundantly.*

Interpretation: Reading wrong theology into the passage. What exactly is abundant living? Luxurious living, or life as the Lord intended it to be lived?

Modeling: How did Jesus live the abundant life? Did any of it have to do with wealth, prestige, or material comfort? Rather, did he not renounce such things?

Dishonesty: Prosperity preachers are crooked. They know very well that the abundant life Jesus promised *and lived* has nothing to do with riches. See 1 Corinthians 1:26–27; 4:1–11).

I was struck when recently re-reading *The Imitation of Christ* (Thomas à Kempis). This passage is apropos:

Many love Jesus so long as no troubles happen to them. Many praise him and bless him, so long as they receive comforts from him. But if Jesus hides himself and seems to withdraw from them for even a little while, they immediately begin complaining or feel a great sense of dejection.... Shouldn't all those constantly seeking his blessing be called mercenaries?[2]

Romans 8:28

And we know that for those who love God all things work together for good, for those who are called according to his purpose.

Context: The Prosperity Gospel does not respect the context of this important passage.

- The verse that follows it is: "For those whom he foreknew he also predestined to be conformed to the image of his Son, in order that he might be the firstborn among many brothers." The "for" indicates that verse 29 is explaining verse 28.

- This is not a promise that in the end we will get our dream job (or dream girl, dream house, etc.). Since the image of Jesus includes much suffering, it means that all things work together for character formation through suffering. Providence isn't unalterable destiny. There isn't necessarily only one right choice when it comes to career, marriage, or residence.

Connection: Misreading this passage easily reinforces "visions and dreams" theology.

IMPACT AND RANGE

Impact:

- Prosperity Theology encourages an infantile focus on physical things.

- It also fuels materialism. This is an ultimately futile cycle: craving for status leads to overspending and debt (Proverbs 22:7).

- This is not following the example of Christ and his disciples!

Range:

- Extremely common among evangelicals.

- Characterizes 95% or more of charismatic churches.[3]

- Normative in Africa, Latin America, much of Asia, and much of North America.

CONCLUDING CHALLENGE

Don't be taken in by this shallow and unbiblical theology, or by the dishonest preachers who, by teaching it, fleece their flocks and fill them with false hopes.

Think critically.

- Read passages in context.
- Don't take the preacher's (or author's) word for it.
- Weigh every claim. Does it make sense biblically?
- Does it fit well with the big picture of biblical theology?

- Dig into the Word!

Resist materialism.

- For our modern society, there is something seductive about Health and Wealth teaching.

- Honor scriptural teaching on wealth and possessions.

- Have nothing to do with materialistic Christianity—for how is this Christian?

- Be a good steward of God's blessings and the fruits of your labor so you can give to those truly in need!

---

1. Further: When I first discovered Jeremiah 29:11–14, I was keen to use it to help believers to seek God. "Hope and a future" is just what they want and need, I thought. How wonderful that God plans to prosper us—that life will be better if we put him first! This is true, yet many readers today go well beyond the meaning of the passage, in the belief that God has a personalized plan, specifically designed for the happiness of each believer. This is simply not true—at least I've never found a scriptural passage that supports it. Many believers take Jeremiah 29 to guarantee a quick blessing—part of our on-demand culture?—but the Lord says the blessing may take generations to be fulfilled. We shouldn't stand around waiting for the blessing to come; we should get on with life and faithfully persevere. (Read the chapter in its entirety, and you may confirm that modern evangelicals have woefully misread this great passage.)

2. Thomas à Kempis, *The Imitation of Christ*, Book 2, chapter 11.

3. Most of the "growth" of Christianity in the developing world is questionable, given that this growth is mainly among charismatic/Pentecostal churches, where the get-rich gospel is driving attendance, financial giving, and numerical growth.

Appendix C
Eight Great Points
to Make with Your Friends

There have been many ideas in this book. Let's boil it all down into a handful of key concepts you can share with others.

1. To begin with, unless there's a God, all morals and values are merely subjective opinions, since *only God is intrinsically good* (Mark 10:18; Micah 6:8a). Ergo, no God, no morality. In the face of any evil, no one can claim, "Hey—that is wrong!" All he can say is, "I don't like it," or "I wish it were otherwise." Morality and God are intimately connected. In studying the tree, we need to take care we don't saw off the branch that is supporting us. This may be too academic a response for most people—though if you are in a university, the point needs to be made frequently!

2. No one can *know* if it is God's desire to eliminate the pain and suffering in this life. Isn't it rather suspicious that we think we can discern God's agenda—one that providentially corresponds neatly with our own? (Job 2:10; Isaiah 55:6–9).

3. Suffering often serves useful functions, after all. What sort of character would we have if life was a nonstop amusement park of pleasure (with free food, and without the lines)? Perseverance through suffering builds character (Romans

5:3–5; James 1:2–3). Both suffering and the sufferer are transformed. As Holocaust survivor Viktor Frankl put it, "In some ways suffering ceases to be suffering at the moment it finds a meaning."[1] It is the believer who has suffered who has the greatest credibility (1 Peter 4:19). As someone else said, "Never trust a Christian who doesn't walk with a limp." (I wish I'd said that.)

4. We live in a moral universe, yet one in which good often goes unrewarded and evil unrequited. Therefore, justice demands, and the Lord will issue, a settling of accounts in the next (Matthew 16:27). It's only by faith in God that we can have assurance that the world isn't monstrously indifferent. The justice we seek and the Judgment Day are inseparable.

5. God understands, and not just because he is all-wise. His understanding of suffering isn't only intellectual, but experiential, for once he walked this earth as one of us. "Because he himself suffered when he was tempted, he is able to help those who are being tempted" (Hebrews 2:18). In God's verbal message to us, the Scriptures, the theme of evil and suffering is ubiquitous. It disturbed Abraham, nonplussed Job, was explained by the prophets, lamented in the Psalms, and clarified in the Apocalypse. Further, if even Jesus Christ had to drink the cup of suffering, why should we imagine we get a free pass? (Romans 8:29; 12:2).

6. Free will is the unique essence of humanity. It's hard to imagine how God could be just in holding us accountable, or even how we could be truly human, in the absence of free will. Yet free will cannot mean only the option to do

good, to live right, and to help others. It must also mean the capacity to do evil, live badly, and hurt others—including the innocent.

7. Christianity offers neither simplistic answers nor escape from pain. The Bible offers no cheap solution to make evil and suffering "all better." But it does speak of a place where God meets us in our suffering, demonstrating that he understands fully. That place is the cross. (Study the cross with your friend, or perhaps read a medical account of the crucifixion.[2]) The Scriptures are deeply nuanced on the topic of suffering. If true faith were an invitation to escape suffering, all the world would be lining up for baptism! Authentic Christianity is an invitation to follow the One who died for us. It means bearing the cross, graciously bearing up under unjust suffering—and all other kinds.

8. You may have met "cotton candy" Christians, whose conviction seems to be that we should smile our way through life without authentic interaction. Yet are you really any different from them—out of touch with reality, leaving it to others to tackle the world's problems? What are *you* doing to alleviate suffering in others' lives? You're either part of the solution or part of the problem (James 2:14–17).

Challenge

Tell your friends what God's word says about the problem of evil. The biblical view connects with our hearts. Many skeptics have been turned off by syrupy expressions of faith. When believers trivialize suffering through sharing scriptures (misapplying them) or offering platitudes, unbelievers feel justified for rejecting our message. But they won't find it so easy to walk away when they hear the realistic diagnosis and gracious solutions found in Scripture.

1. Viktor E. Frankl, *Man's Search for Meaning* (Boston, Massachusetts: Beacon Press, 2006, first published 1946). Frankl explains that despair is suffering without meaning.

2. See https://www.douglasjacoby.com/a-more-accurate-medical-account-of-the-crucifixion/, or the more extensive medical account at https://www.douglasjacoby.com.

Resources for Further Study

Copan, Paul. *Is God a Moral Monster? Making Sense of the Old Testament God.* Grand Rapids, MI: Baker, 2010.

_____ and Matthew Flannagan. *Did God Really Command Genocide? Coming to Terms with the Justice of God.* Grand Rapids, MI: Baker, 2014.

Edwards, Gene. *Exquisite Agony: Healing for Christians Who Have Been Hurt by Other Christians.* Jacksonville, FL: SeedSowers, 1995.

Greig, Pete. *God on Mute: Engaging the Silence of Unanswered Prayer.* Ventura, CA: Regal Books, 2007.

Jacoby, Douglas. *Thrive! Using Psalms to Help You Flourish.* Spring, Texas: IPI, 2014.

_____. Various lessons and Q&A on suffering online at douglasjacoby.com.

Lewis, C. S. *A Grief Observed.* New York, NY: HarperCollins, 1996.

_____. *The Problem of Pain: The Intellectual Problem Raised by Human Suffering, Examined with Sympathy and Realism.* New York, NY: Touchstone, 1996.

MacDonald, James. *When Life Is Hard.* Chicago, IL: Moody, 2010.

Peck, M. Scott. *People of the Lie: The Hope for Healing Human Evil.* New York, NY: Touchstone, 1998.

Piper, John. *Suffering and the Sovereignty of God.* Wheaton, IL: Crossway, 2006.

Russell, Stephen. *Overcoming Evil God's Way: The Biblical and Historical Case for Nonresistance.* Guys Mills, PA: Faith Builders Resource Group, 2008.

Walton, Charlie. *When There Are No Words: Finding Your Way to Cope with Loss and Grief.* Ventura, CA: Pathfinder, 1999.

Wright., N. T. *Evil and the Justice of God.* Downers Grove, IL: Inter-Varsity Press, 2006.

Yancey, Philip. *Disappointment with God: Three Questions No One Asks Aloud.* Grand Rapids, MI: Zondervan, 1997.

_____. *The Jesus I Never Knew.* Grand Rapids, MI: Zondervan, 1995.

_____. *Prayer: Does It Make Any Difference?* New York, NY: Harper-Collins, 2010.

_____. *Reaching for the Invisible God: What Can We Expect to Find?* Grand Rapids, MI: Zondervan, 2000.

_____. *Where Is God When It Hurts?* Grand Rapids, MI: Zondervan, 1997.

Young, William Paul. *The Shack: Where Tragedy Confronts Eternity.* Newbury Park, CA: Windblown Media, 2007.

Zacharias, Ravi. *Deliver Us from Evil: Restoring the Soul in a Disintegrating Culture.* Dallas, TX: Word, 1996.

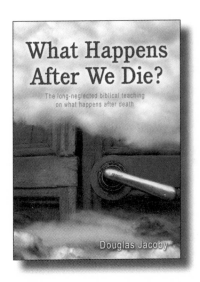

Books
by
Douglas
Jacoby

Available
at
www.ipibooks.com

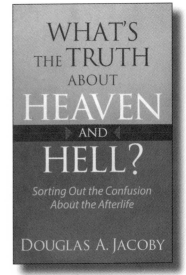

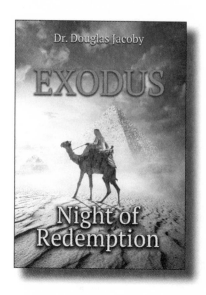

Books
by
Douglas
Jacoby

Available
at
www.ipibooks.com

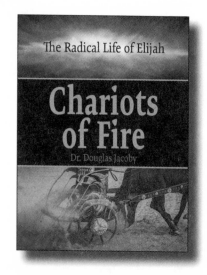

Books
by
Douglas
Jacoby

Available
at
www.ipibooks.com

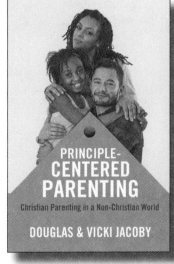

www.ipibooks.com